highlights

KU-344-580

Issue 54 • 3rd quarter 2011

Contents

Issue 54 • 3rd quarter 2011

69

96

THE LOWDOWN

REVIEW

LAST WORD

100

The Philosophers' Magazine,
4 Saddler Street, Durham, DH1 3NP, UK
Tel: 0191 3831 889   Fax: 0191 3862 542
editor@philosophers.co.uk   www.philosophersmag.com

Editor   James Garvey
Editor-in-chief   Julian Baggini
Reviews editor   Jean Kazez
Obituaries   Adam Ferner

Editorial Advisory Board
Miranda Fricker, Simon Glendinning, Daniel D Hutto, Susan James,
David Papineau, Nina Power, Anthony Price, Jonathan Rée,
Richard Schoch, Barry C Smith, Jonathan Wolff

Illustrations/Graphics
Felix Bennett, Adam Ferner, Gareth Southwell

Contributors
Scott Aikin, Deane-Peter Baker, Helen Beebee, Martin Bell,
Ophelia Benson, Thom Brooks, Gregory Currie, Luciano Floridi,
Wendy M Grossman, Mathew Iredale, Troy Jollimore,
Andrew Zimmerman Jones, P J E Kail, Jean Kazez, Neil Levy,
Peter Millican, Dana Nelkin, John Palmer, Tony Pitson,
Elizabeth S Radcliffe, Sam Rickless, Saul Smilansky, Paul Snowdon,
Ernest Sosa, Barry Stroud, Jussi Suikkanen and Robert Talisse

Contributors' Notes
Contact the editor to submit proposals.
Please do not send unsolicited manuscripts.

UK distribution
Central Books, 99 Wallis Road,
London E9 5LN Tel: 020 8985 4854

North America distribution
Source Interlink, 27500 Riverview Center Blvd., Bonita Springs,
Florida 34134 Tel: (239) 949-4450

Printed by
MPG Books Group

Subscriptions
UK: +44 (0) 1442 820580
North America: 1 800 444 2419
See page 13 for full details

Cover
Original artwork by Felix Bennett

from the editor

A few philosophers speak directly to us, and as a result we sometimes form mental pictures of them. It's easy to imagine Hume, red cheeked and pleasingly corpulent, talking us through the arguments after dinner, over a glass of good wine. Nietzsche smiles conspiratorially, blinks and pauses for effect before launching into some new, even more outrageous line of thought. Schopenhauer grimaces, uncomfortable in a chair that's too big for him, spelling out in nauseating detail exactly why this is the worst of all possible worlds. Some philosophers, sometimes, are right there when we read them.

It's easy to think of the Greeks and see long grey beards, bald heads, flowing tunics, maybe sandals covered in the dust of the agora. This is Plato's fault, because his dialogues almost force us to visualise Socrates quizzing some doomed Athenian, right there, in the late afternoon sun. You can become accustomed to thinking of your philosophers in terms of these easy stereotypes, but don't get too comfortable.

Diogenes Laertius, writing in the third century CE, reports that Plato – far from being a wispy sage, gazing off into the heavens, looking beyond this changing, imperfect, filthy world to a reassuringly sanitised realm of being – was once a butch wrestler. "And he learnt gymnastic exercises under the wrestler Ariston of Argos", Diogenes says. "It was by him that he had the name of Plato given to him instead of his original name, on account of his robust figure … There are some also … who say that he wrestled at the Isthmian games."

"Plato", it turns out, is a nickname, perhaps meaning "broad-shouldered". I have no idea why, but discovering this was somehow wonderful, and it changed how I read Plato. He really did live among us in the world, so I started taking him more seriously. There was a muffled cry of horror, however, when Diogenes explained that Aristotle had "very thin legs, they say, and small eyes; but he used to indulge in very conspicuous dress, and rings, and used to dress his hair carefully". I don't mind a philosopher having thin legs and small eyes, but Aristotle the fashionista is too much for me.

Maybe you think that what a philosopher said means more than who they were. I mostly agree with you, but sometimes inside information helps us to understand what they said. I know Pyrrho is an ancient sceptic who held that one might attain an imperturbable peace of mind by suspending judgement on all matters. But I'm not sure I really appreciated the implications and power of his position until I learned this from Diogenes: "He used to clean all the furniture of the house without expressing any annoyance. And it is said that he carried his indifference so far that he even washed a pig."

How many philosophers do you know who are so firm in their convictions that they would wash a pig if that's where the argument leads them?

news

BHL in Libya

FRENCH PHILOSOPHER, ACTIVIST AND CRITIC
Bernard-Henri Lévy might have had an important place in the events leading up to NATO's military intervention in Libya. As Lévy put it in an online forum with readers of *Le Monde*, "My role, I repeat, was extremely simple: bringing to Paris the members of the National Transitional Council; welcoming (opposition leader) Mahmoud Jibril in Paris, the day of the G-8 summit, so that he could plead his case to Hillary Clinton; inviting (opposition envoy) Ali Zeidan to Paris too, the day before yesterday, to present the overview of his project for society to journalists. That's all."

According to some versions of the story, Lévy arrived in Egypt just after the fall of Hosni Mubarak, and found himself drawn to revolutionary events taking off in nearby Libya. With a friend and a photographer in tow, Lévy managed to cross into Libya by catching a ride in a vegetable delivery van. He soon met with representatives of the uprising.

As he said to the *Guardian*, "I told them I can be in contact with Nicolas Sarkozy; we are political adversaries, but I can try to persuade him to see you. What do you think about coming to Paris and meeting the president?" Lévy made several calls on a satellite phone and arranged a meeting between the Libyan opposition and the French President. Lévy told online readers of *Le Monde* that he had no role, "except having had, one evening, in Benghazi, the crazy idea to pick up the phone and call my country's president and recommend that he receive a delegation from Free Libya."

Sarkozy met the delegation and soon afterwards insisted that France recognise them as Libya's legitimate government. Lévy also arranged a meeting with representatives of the Libyan opposition and US Secretary of State Hillary Clinton, who was in Paris at the time for a meeting of the G-8. It's possible this meeting helped incline the US towards military action. By the time the UN voted on air strikes, the US and Britain lined up with France in favour of military action. According to the *New York Times*, Sarkozy phoned Lévy the night of the vote and told him, "We've won".

When asked about his motivations, Lévy told the *Guardian*: "Afterwards there was the reasoning, and that reasoning was that if we let this butcher massacre his own people, the consequences will be terrible not only for Libya but for the region in general. An unpunished Gaddafi would sound a death knell for the Arab spring, the end of this democratic movement and the immense hope it had raised."

Symbols of the Free Libya movement near the court house in Benghazi

© Bernd Brincken

Respite for Keele

FOLLOWING PROTESTS, PETITIONS, LETTERS, and votes, Keele University has scrapped a proposal to close its undergraduate philosophy programme and its centre for professional ethics. The plans were part of a £6.5m university-wide programme of cuts, and while savings of more than £4m were found, a £1.3m gap remained. In addition to cutting the philosophy programmes, efficiency savings of £300,000 from the school of humanities, £250,000 across the faculty of natural sciences, and £100,000 from the school of pharmacy were also proposed.

Instead, the university will find savings in the schools that cover philosophy and the ethics centre, rather than targeting those programmes specifi- cally. Keele philosopher James Tartaglia told the *Times Higher*, "The management agreed that there will be a new intake of students to philosophy next year, and that the proposal … will contain no reference to the closure of either philosophy or (the ethics unit). Savings will still need to be made, but these will be at the school level."

© Jamie Clarke

Keele University chapel

Trouble at Greenwich

ACCORDING TO AN ONLINE PETITION set up by philosophers at Greenwich, "The School of Humanities management announced on March 23rd that recruitment to the Philosophy BA has been stopped, with immediate effect, and that all places on this degree already offered to students for the coming year are to be rescinded. They have further recommended to the University Academic Planning Committee that the Philosophy BA be closed down." The petition in support of Greenwich philosophy has more than 1,000 signatures. A large number of emails from past and present students, as well as academics from around the UK, including the British Philosophy Association and the Society for European Philosophy, are putting pressure on the university to reconsider its decision.

Kathleen Jones, head of philosophy at Greenwich, told *tpm* that "the philosophy team have been invited to a meeting to discuss the situation. This is great news. However, as things stand, there is no agreement to look again at the recruitment issue, but only at the closure. As a number of colleagues from other institutions have noted, without a reversal of the recruitment decision, the closure will happen anyway, just in a rather less overt manner, at the end of the year. The protest thus continues."

UNLV philosophy under threat

THE GOVERNOR OF NEVADA has introduced a budget to the state legislature that allocates $47m less to the University of Nevada, Las Vegas, than in previous years. The university is considering a number of proposals to manage the shortfall, while the governor insists that he will not raise further funds for education through taxes. There are plans to close the departments of philosophy, women's studies and social work.

The executive director of the American Philosophical Association, David E Schrader, said in an open letter that "the elimination of the Philosophy Department would be devastating to the 85 Philosophy Majors and 11 Philosophy faculty members at UNLV ... it is the first case of which I am aware in which a major state university has proposed to eliminate its entire philosophy program."

The chair of the department of philosophy at UNLV, Todd Jones, told *tpm* that "the idea of totally eliminating the department that specialises in teaching students the core ideas of civilization and how to reason well is so outrageous that I am confident that that this particular budget cut proposal will eventually be dropped. But what really needs to change is the mindset behind such proposals. America has long been a country where, if a bridge needed building, the community built it. If education needed funding, the community funded it. We need to get back to that fundamental ethic of taking care of each other and away from mindlessly insisting that there can never be new taxes on anybody, no matter how wealthy, or for any project, no matter how important."

Good news from Twin Earth

HILARY PUTNAM, Cogan University Professor Emeritus in the Department of Philosophy at Harvard, has been awarded the Rolf Schock Prize in Logic and Philosophy by the Royal Swedish Academy. The triennial prizes are awarded in the fields of logic and philosophy, mathematics, the visual arts and musical arts. Each prize is worth about £50,000. Past winners include W V O Quine, Michael Dummett, John Rawls, Saul Kripke and Thomas Nagel. According to the Academy, Putnam won for "his contribution to the understanding of semantics for theoretical and 'natural kind' terms, and of the implications of this semantics for philosophy, theory of knowledge, philosophy of science and metaphysics".

© Hilary Putnam

Hilary Putnam

Air Force recruits a metaphysician

THE US AIR FORCE has asked Stephen Mumford, professor of philosophy at the University of Nottingham, to join a group working on change in complex systems. Working alongside engineers, economists, defence contractors, physicists, lawyers and cognitive scientists, Mumford is part of a research project called "Understanding and Influencing the Causality of Change in Complex Socio-Technical Systems". The effort is partly underwritten by the US Air Force Office of Scientific Research, and the project will be conducted by the Asian Office of Aerospace Research and Development, based in Tokyo.

Mumford works on the metaphysics of science, on such topics as causation, the laws of nature, properties and possibility. His work aims to unify and explain these things in terms of real dispositions or powers. In a forthcoming book called *Getting Causes from Powers*, co-authored with Rani Lill Anjum, Mumford spells out a conception of causation which takes account of complexity and context-sensitivity. Most accounts of cause, they argue, begin with the thought that if one thing is the cause of another, then the first should always be followed by the second. This, they say, fails to take into account the complex phenomena that arise when multiple causes combine.

We ignore the combination of multiple causes at our peril. As Mumford put it in a press release, "A factor that in one context can cause a certain effect might in another have the opposite effect. In medicine, for instance, drugs that tend to produce a health benefit can do the opposite when combined in certain ways. We should not understand causal production in isolated chunks but as interrelated and holistic."

As he goes on to explain, "Philosophers often take regularity as the starting point for theories of causation. Once we recognise the significance of complexity, we see that A may tend towards B, and often succeed in producing it, but cannot deliver a regularity. When combined with a further factor C, A might tend away from B."

It is unclear what pay-off the project will have. "There might be no practical outcome of the research for decades," he told *tpm*, "but we know that many great advances have started this way."

© DrPete/flickr

In memoriam

SUSAN LESLIE CAMPBELL died on 12 February 2011 at the age of 54.

Born in Edmonton in 1957, Campbell completed her undergraduate and graduate degrees in philosophy at the University of Alberta. She received her doctorate from the University of Toronto in 1992 and became a member of the philosophy department and the gender and women's studies program at Dalhousie University soon after.

Her philosophical interests were wide and varied – embodiment, emotions, race and racism, conceptions of authenticity, and agency – but of her contributions, her work on memory is of particular note. In a number of papers and books, most recently *Relational Remembering: Rethinking the Memory Wars* – which was awarded the Social Philosophy Book Prize in 2003 – she examines the different manifestations, and social role, of the Anglo-European conception of memory. Unlike much of the dry analytic work on the subject – which reduces experiential memory to little more than a logical relation – Campbell considered the social repercussions of a memory-based theory of personhood. Specifically, she investigated how, when individuals are discredited as rememberers – for example, in cases of domestic abuse – they are, by that model, undermined as persons.

Although broad in scope, a common theme of her work was a concern with the societal issues raised by contemporary anglophone philosophy. Whether engaging in feminist critique, or considering the much-neglected issue of racism, or racial diversity in philosophy, Campbell was one of the few philosophers who demonstrated an acute awareness of the shortcomings of the discipline as it is practised today.

She is survived by her partner, Jan Sutherland, and her sisters Katy and Lori.

JOHN ACHESON FARIS, emeritus professor of philosophy at the Queen's University of Belfast, died on 26 February 2011 at the age of 97. He was born in Caledon, County Tyrone in 1913, and was educated at the Royal School Dungannon, before attending Worcester College, Oxford, to study philosophy. After graduation he became an assistant lecturer at Queen's, where he continued for the rest of his career, interrupted only by his service with the Royal Artillery during the Second World War.

Faris published primarily on mathematical logic; his *Truth-Functional Logic* and *Quantification Theory* stand as staples on university reading lists. But his interests extended beyond purely formal logic, and he had a particular interest in the paradoxes of ancient Greek philosophy. In *The Paradoxes of Zeno* he combines a careful analysis of fifth century BCE texts with an understanding of the latest mathematical and physical theories of time and motion, to shed light on ancient puzzles.

In an obituary on Queen's website, a friend and colleague, Jonathan Gorman, describes Faris as "the kindest and most thoughtful of men … (whose) gentleness and great clarity of mind remained with him until the end." He is survived by his wife, Mary Josephine, and their four sons, George, Neil, John and Paul.

IAN KIDD, emeritus professor of Greek at St Andrews University, died on 20 March 2011, aged 89.

Born in French India in 1922, Kidd's parents sent him to Dundee at the age of five to be raised by his grandparents. His academic excellence at school assured him a place at St Andrews, but in 1942 he was commissioned as lieutenant in the Argyll and Sutherland Highlanders, and left his studies to serve in North Africa and Italy.

He returned to St Andrews in 1945, and graduated two years later, before taking a further classics degree at Queen's College, Oxford.

Kidd spent almost forty years at St Andrews, as professor of ancient philosophy, and Greek, and produced notable contributions to the study of Plato, and Stoicism. Of his work, his commentary and translation of the fragments of the Stoic, Posidonius, is perhaps best known, demonstrating, as it does, his polymathic grasp of ancient history, geography, physics and ethics.

He is survived by his three sons, Anthony, Robin and Simon.

SARA ("SALLY") ELIZABETH RUDDICK (née Loop) died on 20 March 2011 at the age of 76.

Ruddick was born in Toledo, Ohio in 1935. She received her bachelor's degree in philosophy at Vassar in 1957, and her doctorate from Harvard seven years later. For almost forty years she worked at The New School for Social Research, in New York.

Best known for research on mothering and child-care, Ruddick's book *Maternal Thinking: Toward a Politics of Peace* is credited with encouraging a significant shift in philosophical approaches to maternity. Where motherhood had once been considered simply a passive biological function, Ruddick oriented it around the practice and activities of child-rearing, thereby construing it as sex-neutral. She argued that the education and nurture of children affects the parent as much as the child, as well as stimulating certain cognitive and ethical capacities, for example a resistance to militarism and violence.

Ruddick was an ethicist whose philosophy was manifest in her manner towards colleagues and students. Writing for the blog "Probe – Create Change – Reflect", Peter J Taylor quotes a friend at The New School who knew her well: "it was beyond the realm of possibility that she could treat anyone in any way other than with total respect and regard". She is survived by her husband William, their children Hal and Elizabeth, and four grandchildren.

Peter Adamson

Ian Kidd

mediawatch

Philosophy and philosophers in the mass media

Once upon a time, not so long ago, no one thought that there was a mind-body problem. No one thought consciousness was a special mystery and they were right.

Galen Strawson, *Observer*, 9 January

We cannot master happiness, it cannot be the fruit of our decisions. We have to be more humble. Not because we should praise frailty or humility but because people are very unhappy when they try hard and fail. We have a lot of power in our lives but not the power to be happy. Happiness is more like a moment of grace.

Pascal Bruckner, *Observer*, 23 January

The cynical wisdom of western liberals, according to which, in Arab countries, genuine democratic sense is limited to narrow liberal elites while the vast majority can only be mobilised through religious fundamentalism or nationalism, has been proven wrong.

Slavoj Žižek, CiF, *Guardian*, 1 February

Life, morality and politics are not science, but their improvement requires thought – not only thought about the most effective means of shaping people … but thought about what our ends should be.

Thomas Nagel, *New York Times*, 11 March

The real test of democratic citizenship is the ability to engage in reasoned moral argument including reasoned disagreement in public.

Michael Sandel, *Gainesville Sun*, 22 March

I am just doing my work. I believe that in a normal, civilised, adult democracy an intellectual should be able to speak to a political leader.

Bernard-Henri Lévy, *Observer*, 27 March

If the ideas on our agenda happen to overlap with things the government wants to talk about, fine. But for us to be put in the position where something that wasn't on our agenda is now painted as being a strategic priority for the academy, then what the hell is going on?

James Ladyman, *Times Higher*, 28 March

We have a responsibility to live well. Our challenge is to act as if we respect ourselves. Enjoying ourselves is not enough.

Ronald Dworkin, *Guardian*, 31 March

What would happen if the Nato forces really took seriously the idea of the equal value of all human life? They would then have to compensate Afghans for the civilian deaths and injuries they are causing at the same level as they would compensate their own citizens.

Peter Singer, CiF, *Guardian*, 1 April

How can you be a militant atheist? How can you be a militant non-stamp collector? This is really what it comes down to. You just don't collect stamps. So how can you be a Fundamentalist non-stamp collector? It's like sleeping furiously. It's just wrong.

A C Grayling, *Guardian*, 3 April

tpm
the philosophers' magazine

WAYS TO ORDER
ONLINE AT WWW.TPMAGORA.COM

IN NORTH AMERICA ONLY
1. Complete the order form using the appropriate $ prices
2. Send orders to:
   The Philosophers' Magazine
   c/o The Philosophy Documentation Center
   PO Box 7147
   Charlottesville, VA 22906-7147
   USA
Or phone 1-800-444-2419, or fax (434) 220 3301

IN THE UK AND REST OF THE WORLD
1. Complete the order form using the appropriate £ prices for
   where you live
2. Send orders to:
   tpm – The Philosophers' Magazine
   Unit 8, The Old Silk Mill
   Brook Street
   Tring
   Hertfordshire
   HP23 5EF, UK
Or phone 01442 820580, or fax 01442 827912

All prices include postage and packing
Please allow up to 28 days for delivery

Order form

Please start my subscription to TPM.

I enclose a cheque/PO for _____ made payable to
Acumen Publishing Ltd, or debit my credit card

☐ Visa   ☐ Mastercard   ☐ Switch   ☐ Discover

Card number: _____

Expiry date: ____/____ Signature: _____

Issue no. (Switch only): _____

3-digit card security number: _____

Name: _____

Address: _____

_____

_____

Post/Zip code: _____ Country: _____

How not to argue
The uses and abuses of argument

Fact and fiction
Interview with Rebecca Goldstein

PLUS Peter Hacker interview · Fair votes · The Plato Code · The Python rematch · Green conference · News ·olumns · Reviews

Experimental philosophy
 it time to burn e armchair?

umanities der threat
 erview with tha Nussbaum

PLUS Toby Young interview · Simon Blackburn on the offensive · Soldiers' morality · Philosopher politicians · Emotional computers · Wizards · News · Columns · Reviews

THOUGHT PROVOKING THOUGHTS

PRICE LIST

SINGLE COPY UK	£5.99
SUBSCRIPTION 1 YR UK	£19.99
SINGLE COPY US	$9.99
SUBSCRIPTION 1YR US	$34.99
SUBSCRIPTION 1 YR EUROPE	£23.99
SUBSCRIPTION 1 YR ROW	£27.99
INSTITUTION SUB UK	£59.99
INSTITUTION SUB EUROPE	£63.99
INSTITUTION SUB ROW	£67.99

Ophelia Benson
threads

Sexual harassment in philosophy

The blog What is it Like to be a Woman in Philosophy? (beingawomaninphilosophy.wordpress.com) has a section devoted to sexual harassment in the profession. In late March, Mark Lance, John Protevi and Eric Schliesser wrote a post at the blog New APPS: Art, Politics, Philosophy, Science (newappsblog.com) on how difficult it is to do anything about sexual harassment. "Institutional mechanisms provide little in the way of redress to the victims of such figures. Those who have been harassed, or worse, come forward in many cases, put themselves through a long and painful process, and if the figure is prominent it is very unlikely that any meaningful action will be taken. Given this systematic failure of formal mechanisms, it should not come us a surprise that many women get discouraged and drop out of the discipline along the way."

What, they asked, is to be done? The obvious response to a failure of formal mechanisms is to try informal ones. "We believe there are informal sanctions that could make a difference. The Feminist Philosophers blog recently suggested not inviting serial harassers to conferences. One could easily extend this to not inviting them to publish, not conversing with them at conferences, advising students to avoid their graduate program, etc." There are obvious problems with such informal social sanctions, but there are also problems with doing nothing. Comments were invited, and received.

Scott Jaschik did a long story at Inside Higher Education (insidehighered.com/home), quoting Mark Lance saying "that over 25 years of teaching philosophy, he has become 'completely disillusioned' with the way colleges handle complaints. Before coming to Georgetown, he saw a case in which he had direct evidence of the accusations being 'open and shut', but the professor received only 'a slap on the wrist'."

Lance said that "of course" one has to be careful about believing unsubstantiated rumours. But he noted that what he and his colleagues are calling for isn't sending anyone to jail.

Jaschik also interviewed Peggy DesAutels, associate professor of philosophy at the University of Dayton and chair of the American Philosophical Association's Committee on Women, who said the discussion is long overdue. DesAutels said she personally could

Ophelia Benson is editor of butterfliesandwheels.com and co-author of *Why Truth Matters* (Continuum, 2006)

"There are well-known, famous, serial harassers"

verify that some of the top philosophers in academe have mistreated many women over the years. "There are well known, famous, serial harassers", she said. And she said that most women in philosophy have seen firsthand that famous philosophers don't seem to pay a price for the way they treat women. "To the degree that they are famous, they move from university to university", she said.

Part of the problem is that the number of women in philosophy is still low. In a circumstance that would not be possible in other humanities disciplines, "there are departments that have no feminist influence and very few women and that are very treacherous for women."

A commenter, "Jeanne", observed that "The practice of ignoring sexual harassment, and hence being complicit with sexual harassment, is deeply institutionalized in philosophy. This institutionalization is so strong that the costs or perceived costs of making a formal complaint are often prohibitive. Note, those costs include shunning. Formal policies are of no use if the culture and practices of a group push people not to use them."

She went on to describe her experience: "In dealing with my own case of sexual harassment I was told in no uncertain terms that I was welcome to follow the official channels and raise a complaint, but I needed to think carefully about what my job would be like whether or not the complaint was successful (no one seemed to wonder what my job was like with a harasser down the hall and a group of colleagues who knew it). And, I was further told that it was a very real possibility that my complaint would not be successful (this even though the capping event happened in front of a dozen philosophy professors). So, yah, we have a great anti-harassment policy. Our administrators are proud of the quality of that policy. But, the culture and practices of the institution make it worse than ineffective, because it allows folks to blame me for not using it."

David Velleman, however, commented on the original article, "OK – I'll be the Bad Guy (emphasis on 'Guy'). Sexual harassment in the workplace is a grave and urgent problem. At the same time, the solution being proposed here is a blacklist, and history has taught us that blacklists are extremely dangerous. An instrument of social discipline with such a tragic history should not be used to address even grave and urgent problems." An "Anonymous" (there were many of those on all four posts, for [probably] obvious reasons) replied to Velleman that "These sorts of informal practices can be dangerous, sure. But sometimes the benefits outweigh the dangers. So, e.g., it's presumably true of the profession, right now, that a philosopher repeatedly accused of making racist remarks would be widely shunned. This practice has its dangers (people can always be misunderstood, falsely accused, etc.); but it seems like a good thing overall. How (genuine question) would the proposed practice be any different?"

There the discussion rested ... for the moment.

Handling a 1787 French translation of Hobbes's *Oeuvres Philosophiques et Politiques*, its paper a little dirty-looking through age, I have to confess it's hard not fall in love a little with it.

Great books

JULIAN BAGGINI TAKES STOCK OF THE TRADE IN RARE PHILOSOPHY BOOKS

I haven't read John Locke's *Essay Concerning Human Understanding* since I was an undergraduate, and I already have a copy. Nevertheless, the desire to own the edition of it I have in my hands is very strong indeed. The clue to my otherwise inexplicable craving comes in the bookseller's description: "The paper is crisp, it's clean, it's readable, it's a handsome book." This is not the way we often talk about books these days, but then this is not a contemporary printing. It is in fact a 1694 second edition of the *Essay*, which added thirty-one pages to the first, as well as a handsome portrait of the author. At £2,000 (about $3,000), it's a bargain I can't afford.

Philosophy is often seen as a repository of great books, but we tend not to think about how that treasure trove is actually built on solid, physical, historical artefacts. There is a niche trade in these books, and I recently caught up with two of Britain's long-established leaders in the field to find out how it works and who keeps it going.

Rachel Lee and Herb Tandree both run antiquarian and second-hand book businesses, specialising in philosophy. Both used to work for Rudi Thoemmes, former publisher and still an antiquarian bookseller focusing on the history of ideas. That the three of them lead the field in the UK reflects the small nature of the world they inhabit.

Tandree started out as an academic, but Lee fell into her specialised subject by accident, simply because it was what she learned about under Thoemmes. "I have read some of my philosophy books, but I have to say a lot of them aren't the easiest things in the world to take in", she says. "I'm perhaps more interested in the history of philosophy, how some books relate to

Julian Baggini is editor-in-chief of *tpm* and author of *The Ego Trick: What Does it Mean to Be You?* (Granta, 2011)

each other, what comes of those books, the criticisms of those books and the bigger history."

Given that these books often sell for thousands of pounds, who's buying them? Lee says that at the moment her main customers for high-end books are archives at universities, sadly not often in Britain, but in America, Europe and, to a declining extent, Japan. Private collectors also play a significant role, coming in two general types: people who collect books of a particular author or era, and academics who collect in their special subjects.

What is it, though, that makes one book worth more than another? "It depends on the buyer", says Tandree. "There's a whole use factor: I need that in order to study or to research. And then there's the collecting aspect. A collector wants a first edition or a second edition because of, say, a textual change." As with any antiquarian business, although the fundamentals are the usual market forces of supply and demand, because both are being powered by a small number of forces, small variations can make all the difference between whether something is hard to get hold of or relatively easy to come by. That is why

Rachel Lee and Herb Tandree

the internet still leaves a role for a specialised, expert bookseller.

In general terms, the internet has transformed bookselling. On the one hand, it has broadened the customer base for sellers considerably. It used to be the case that only people who even knew what books a dealer had for sale were those who were either on a snail-mailing list for a catalogue or who came into your shop, if you

"A few years ago I sold the collection of Iris Murdoch"

had one. Now, in theory, anyone in the world can find a book with a careful Google search. This opening up has a downside too: booksellers are now in direct competition with everyone else in the world who sells the same or similar books, and this drives prices down.

There are nonetheless opportunities for specialist booksellers to make the most of their unique knowledge base. The web can only set the price if there are enough of the products out there to set a benchmark. "The scarcer something is, the easier to use your knowledge and what you've learned over twenty, thirty, forty, years", says Lee. "If there's no copy on the internet, your gut reaction comes into it and you think, I think I could get this amount for it or I don't know how much I'll get for it."

Tandree explains that another opportunity is that "in specialist selling you can have what nobody else has". If you have the only copy of a book available for sale in the whole world at that time, someone looking for it will find you and will probably know they can't go elsewhere.

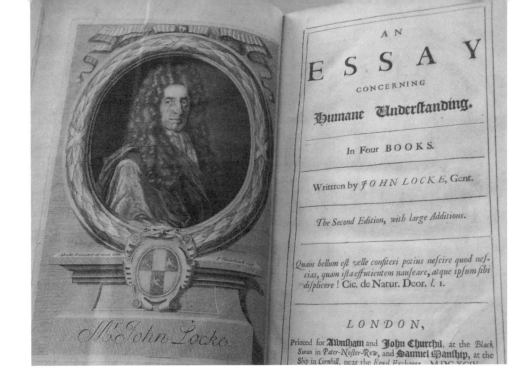

Take as an example one of the most valuable single items to have passed through Lee's hands, a copy of Wittgenstein's *Tractatus* in its first incarnation in a German periodical in 1921. "That's quite scarce. and I think I sold that for £10,000. It doesn't look like anything at all – it's a twentieth-century pamphlet in wrappers."

Another service that specialist sellers uniquely offer is the sale of collections. "Mostly by collection we mean the collection that has been put together over the lifetime of an academic", explains Lee. "Very often it's on one subject, it's very specialised, the books all interlinked in some way that they relate to each other."

"Sometimes I'll do subject collections, on moral philosophy or logic, and these are aimed at libraries", says Tandree. But why do libraries buy whole collections like these rather than simply select the individual books they want? "Time", is his short answer. "Librarians are like any other profession, terribly overworked, and the building of collections in research libraries has suffered for the last twenty years. The main thing is you save them time."

Some collections are a little more special. "A few years ago I sold the collection of Iris Murdoch," says Lee, "and although it was mentioned a number of times that perhaps that collection should have been split, so that everybody should have the chance to own something that once belonged to Iris Murdoch, I felt very strongly it should be kept together because the books were related to each other, and they were books that she used in writing her philosophy books and her novels." Murdoch had written lots of notes in these books, so perhaps it is good that the collection eventually went to Kingston University in London and now makes up part of the Centre for Iris Murdoch Studies. The university paid £120,000 for the archive, proceeds from which went to establish the Iris Murdoch scholarship at St Anne's College, Oxford, where Murdoch tutored between 1948 and 1963.

There is certainly a romance to the old book trade. "People come into my office and they love the smell," says Lee. "I don't notice it anymore but they say it smells lovely, it smells of old books." Handling a 1787 French translation of Hobbes's

Œuvres Philosophiques et Politiques, its paper a little dirty-looking through age, I have to confess it's hard not fall in love a little with it. "Aesthetically, they're lovely to handle. They have portraits, often they have an earlier owner's comments in the margins, the beautiful leather bindings …"

Given how wonderful they are, don't the sellers get attached to them and reluctant to give them up? Interestingly, neither Tandree nor Lee can name a single book they just couldn't bear to sell on. "You have to learn first that you have to let things go", says Tandree. "When I first started selling books I said to Rudi Thoemmes, how can you let these things go? And of course, being an old hand at it, there was no answer, and I realised the answer to my question was that over time, you're in the business of selling books."

"Aesthetically, they're lovely to handle"

It is the fate of all these books that they find an owner, not just a dealer. "I was once told I was naive to thinking there was somebody somewhere for every book," says Lee, "but I still think that."

> **LINKS**
>
> Rachel Lee Rare Books,
> www.rachelleerarebooks.co.uk
>
> Herb Tandree Philosophy Books,
> www.philosophy-books.co.uk
>
> Rudi Thoemmes Rare Books, www.rrbltd.co.uk

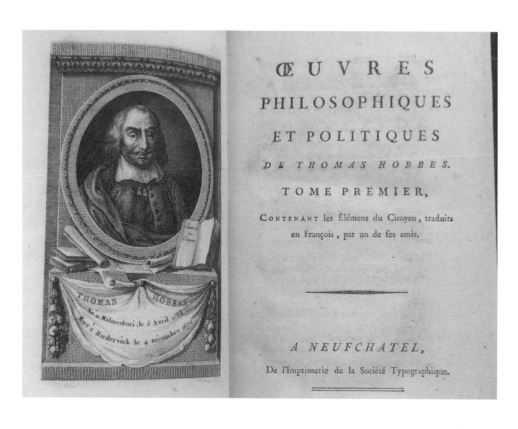

Luciano Floridi
word of mouse

Enveloping the world for AI

t is a well-known fact that AI research seeks both to *reproduce* the outcome of our intelligent behaviour by non-biological means, and to *produce* the non-biological equivalent of our intelligence. As a branch of engineering interested in *intelligent behaviour reproduction*, AI has been astoundingly successful. We increasingly rely on AI-related applications (smart technologies) to perform tasks that would be simply impossible by un-aided or un-augmented human intelligence. But as a *branch of cognitive science interested in intelligence production*, AI has been a dismal disappointment. Productive AI does not merely underperform with respect to human intelligence; it has not joined the competition yet. The fact that Watson – IBM's system capable of answering questions asked in natural language – recently outperformed its human opponents when playing *Jeopardy!* only shows that artefacts can be smart without being intelligent.

Productive and reproductive AI have often engaged in fratricidal feuds for intellectual predominance, academic power and financial resources. That is partly because they both claim common ancestors and a single intellectual inheritance: a founding event, the Dartmouth Summer Research Conference on Artificial Intelligence in 1956, and a founding father, Alan Turing, with his machine and its computational limits, and then his famous test. It hardly helps that a simulation might be used in order to check both whether the simulated source has been produced, and whether the targeted source's behaviour or performance has been reproduced or even surpassed. The misalignment of their goals and results has caused endless and mostly pointless diatribes. Defenders of AI point to the strong results of reproductive AI, whereas detractors of AI point to the weak results of productive AI. Many of the current speculations on the so-called singularity issue – reflection on the possibility of engineered, superhuman intelligence – have their roots in such confusion.

In order to escape the dichotomy just outlined, one needs to realise that AI cannot be reduced to a "science of nature", or to a "science of culture", because it is a "science of the artificial", as Herbert Simon puts it. As such, AI pursues neither a *descriptive* nor a *prescriptive* approach to the world. Instead, AI investigates the conditions that make it possible to build artefacts that

Luciano Floridi (philosophyofinformation.net) holds the research chair in philosophy of information at the University of Hertfordshire and is president of the International Association for Computing and Philosophy

are embedded in the world and interact with it successfully. In other words, AI *inscribes* the world, for such artefacts are new, logico-mathematical pieces of code, that is, new texts, written in Galileo's mathematical book of nature.

Until recently, the widespread impression was that such process of adding to the mathematical book of nature required the feasibility of productive AI. After all, developing even a rudimentary form of non-biological intelligence may seem to be not only the best but perhaps the only way to implement technologies sufficiently adaptive and flexible to deal effectively with a complex, ever-changing and often unpredictable and unfriendly environment.

Such an impression is not incorrect, but it is distracting, because, while we were unsuccessfully pursuing the inscription of productive AI into the world, we were actually re-ontologising the world to fit reproductive AI. The world is becoming an infosphere increasingly well-adapted to AI's limited capacities. In robotics, an *envelope* is the three-dimensional space that defines the boundaries that a robot can reach. We have been enveloping the world for decades without fully realising it.

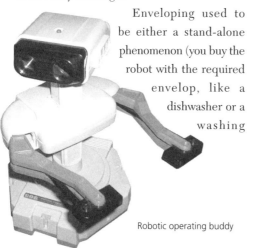

Enveloping used to be either a stand-alone phenomenon (you buy the robot with the required envelop, like a dishwasher or a washing

© Caleb Goessling

Robotic operating buddy

machine) or implemented within the walls of industrial buildings. Nowadays, enveloping the environment into an AI-friendly infosphere pervades many aspects of reality and is visible almost everywhere. If driverless vehicles can move around with decreasing trouble, this is not because productive AI has finally arrived, but because the "around" they need to negotiate has become increasingly suitable to reproductive AI.

Enveloping is a trend that is robust, cumulative and progressively refining. It has nothing to do with some sci-fi singularity, for it is not based on some unrealistic (as far as our current and foreseeable understanding of AI and computing is concerned) speculations about some super AI taking over the world in the near future. But it is a process that raises the risk that our technologies might shape our physical and conceptual environments and constrain us to adjust to them because that is the best, or sometimes the only, way to make things work.

By becoming more critically aware of the re-ontologising power of reproductive AI and smart applications, we might be able to avoid the worst forms of distortion (when the re-ontologising is too human-unfriendly), or at least be consciously tolerant of the effects of such technologies, especially while waiting for a better design. In the latter case, being able to imagine what the future will be like and what adaptive demands technologies will place on their human users may help to devise technological solutions that can lower their anthropological costs. In short, intelligent design should play a major role in shaping the future of our interactions with forthcoming technological artefacts. After all, it is a sign of intelligence to make stupidity work for you.

"Even the statement 'There are no such things as moral duties' is a claim about moral duties. There is no neutral position. If I say, 'Are there any such things as moral duties?' and you say, 'No', you're not being neutral. You're making a decision. You're deciding that rich people have no duty to help poor people. That's what you're saying."

Diamonds in the cosmic sands

RONALD DWORKIN TELLS JAMES GARVEY WHY OUR THOUGHTS ABOUT LIVING WELL, BEING GOOD, TRUTH, BEAUTY AND JUSTICE MUST STAND OR FALL TOGETHER

You might think about the importance of good consequences when you decide to give money to help the victims of an earthquake. Perhaps you look to yet another set of values when you make decisions about the kind of life you want to live. Still more principles might come to mind when you wonder whether the cuts a government makes to its welfare budget are unjust. Maybe other values lie behind your smile when you think about how beautiful a sunset is. If you're like most people, you think that judgements about politics, morality, living well, truth,

James Garvey is editor of *tpm*

beauty and so on depend on separate, disconnected values. If you're like most people, Ronald Dworkin disagrees with you.

As a Greek parable has it, the fox knows many different things, but the hedgehog knows one big thing. Dworkin is a hedgehog, and the one big thing he knows is that value is unified. As he puts it in his new book, *Justice for Hedgehogs*, "The truth about living well and being good and what is wonderful is not only coherent but mutually supporting: what we think about any one of these must stand up, eventually, to any argument we find compelling about the rest." If Dworkin is right about this, then every one of the thoughts we have about what matters to us is interconnected, unified and independent of the world of

scientific fact. The view puts him at odds with almost everyone engaged in moral and political philosophy.

Many philosophers think, for example, that it's at least reasonable to say that we can't sensibly talk about what values are without considering different questions, such as "Are there values? Is there any such thing as goodness?" Philosophy

"The debate between me and Hart is more nuanced than people take it"

books begin with chapters addressing just those questions. What's wrong with starting there before we go on to questions of value proper?

"I think it's a mistake to think that those are different kinds of question," Dworkin says, settling into a couch in his Belgravia home. I waded through a sea of plummy accents, spectacularly expensive houses and Land Rovers on my way here, but Dworkin is comfortable in his skin and unaffected. Urbane, but not so you'd notice.

"The idea is that there are two kinds of questions. 'Are there any such things as values?', and then if the answer is yes you can start talking about other questions, questions about what the values are. I think there's only one kind of question, which is about what the values are. You might give a negative answer, you might say there are no values, but you have to defend that answer in the same way that you would defend the answer, 'This is beautiful' or 'That's immoral'. It would be a mistake to think that there's a prior, separate kind of question."

There is another foxy mistake out there too. Given that so many people disagree when it comes to moral matters, how can we say we're right and others are wrong without finding some neutral perspective? It only takes a moment to notice that a neutral perspective is impossible. Morality looks alarmingly relative.

"That line of thought is very popular," Dworkin says, "and it's wrong, because it just assumes that there's a way to talk about these things which is not itself committed. But there is no such way. Even the statement 'There are no such things as moral duties' is a claim about moral duties. There is no neutral position. If I say 'Are there any such things as moral duties?' and you say 'No', you're not being neutral. You're making a decision. You're deciding that rich people have no duty to help poor people. That's what you're saying."

How does Dworkin respond to perhaps the foxiest proposition of all: that we can't decide moral questions by simply repeating our value judgements? That's begging the question, one might think, so we need something other than value to ground value. We have to look outside of morality, to metaphysics or epistemology, to find a foundation for morality.

"It's a mistake to think that. It supposes that there's something you can say, for example about moral duties, which doesn't itself make a moral claim. You can say, for example, 'Moral judgements aren't true or false, they just express an emotional commitment.' That's saying something which many people believe isn't itself a moral judgement. They say it's a statement *about* moral judgements. But the idea that there can be some claim about the truth or falsity of moral judgements which is not itself a moral judgement is a mistake."

Dworkin thinks that it's wrong to look for something other than value to shore up our value judgements. He argues for the independence of value, insisting that values depend on values – we must not try to support them with premises arising in the world of fact and measurement. As he says in his book, "We need a new revolution. We must make the world of science safe for value."

Moral judgements are made true not by something in the world, according to Dworkin, but by an adequate moral argument for their truth – and it's adequate moral arguments all the way down. I ask him what he says to someone who finds that unsatisfying, who thinks it's viciously circular.

"Think about what the other opinions are. What would someone think who disagrees with me? One might say that moral judgements aren't made true by anything, because they're not true. Maybe they're not the kind of thing that can be true, like emotional outbursts. That's one view, and it's wrong, and we can have an argument about that."

"Someone else might say that some moral judgements are true, and when they are true they're made true by something real, something out there, some moral particle ... 'morons'. If you think that, then you have no reason to deny that there are fundamental conflicts of value. If moral judgements are made true by morons, there could be different kinds of morons. But that's very silly, because there are no such things as morons, but that is a view you could have."

"At this point an interesting epistemological question arises, which might explain why some people find my view unsatisfying. If, as I say, there aren't things out there in virtue of which some moral propositions are true, then how can we have any reason to think moral judgements are true? If I'm right in thinking that murder is wrong, then my being right is only an accident. In some way or other it's true, but there's no connection to my thinking it's true. The only way you can

"We must make the world of science safe for value"

get a connection is by supposing there's something real, something out there, which is having an impact on me, something responsible for my thinking that murder is wrong. Murder really is wrong, so someone might think that there *has* to be a connection between its being wrong and my thinking it's wrong. The kind of thing I say about there being an interpretive argument doesn't display a connection of the right kind, so people can be distracted by that."

Dworkin's claim that we can arrive at objectivity through interpretation is intriguing, and it's connected in his thinking to the notion that all value is independent and unified. He explains, "The only way to argue for a moral proposition or any proposition about value – beauty and ethics included – is to make another claim about value. If that's true, then, as long as you're defending any claim about value, you are making other claims about value, and that can only be the case if there's support in every part of what you think, about what's good and beautiful and the rest of it. It means there are no conflicts, no genuine or basic conflicts in the truth about values."

He puts that carefully, and he should. It's easy to misconstrue. He's not saying that there are no conflicts about value. People argue about what's right and wrong and find themselves troubled by moral dilemmas all the time. What he means is that there are no real conflicts in *the truth* about value.

Critics have pressed Dworkin on this point. Imagine that a colleague asks you to comment on

"There are no conflicts in the truth about values"

a draft of his book, and you think it's bad. You'll be cruel if you're frank but a liar if you're not. For Dworkin, the conflict can only be apparent. There has to be a way to resolve the tension, show that the conflict is only superficial, and find an answer.

"Moral concepts are works in progress," Dworkin says. "Consider what you actually do in cases like this. Suppose you think about it, and you tell your colleague that the book is pretty good. You now think that's the right thing to do, because you have refined at least one of your concepts. That's the best way to explain what you did. You might have said to yourself, 'Well, it isn't *really* being dishonest if I tell him his book is pretty good.' You've thought more about what honesty is. That's my description of what happened."

"What's the other description? Do we really say, 'I've got two values, and I've got to choose between them.' On what basis can you choose between them? If they're out there like morons, pulling at you, and you're not trying to interpret them, how could you choose between them?

You'd have to say that one is more important than the other. Why? Is there some third value that you're using to choose? As these things present themselves to us it looks like a conflict, but even if I accept that, it doesn't follow that there isn't a right or wrong thing to do. If that doesn't follow, then you have to think the conflict isn't genuine or deep. You must treat it as work to be done, work in progress."

The thought that there is an objectively correct answer to moral questions, and the further thought that one can arrive at it through a process of interpretation, sound like an expansion of views first scouted by Dworkin in the philosophy of law. He argues that the ideal judge, Judge Hercules, who is in possession of a great store of wisdom, a full command of the law, and plenty of time, would always come to the one right answer in deciding a case. Is his defence of the unity of value an expansion of these sorts of thoughts in the philosophy of law?

"I first developed this approach when I was thinking about law. I started as a Wall Street lawyer, running around the world making money for other people. I went to law school, I was a lawyer, so I began to think about the law. As time went on I realised that the problems of legal reasoning are not special – they're problems over the whole domain of value. I began to think that all of these things are united."

Dworkin clerked for Judge Learned Hand, then 87 years old, and accounts by Dworkin and others of their exchanges suggest that it was an incredibly exciting and intellectually stimulating time. Dworkin tucks a feel for Hand's personality into a footnote to a collection of papers. He recalls Hand's vision of his first day in heaven. In the morning, there's a baseball

game, the bases are loaded, it's the bottom of the ninth, Hand hits a home run and wins the game. In the afternoon, with a minute left to play in an American football match, Hand catches the ball and sprints down the sideline to victory. There's a banquet in the evening, with the greatest minds in history assembled – Socrates, Descartes and Voltaire among them. Voltaire rises to give the after dinner speech, and after a few words from him his audience erupts, "Shut up Voltaire, and sit down. WE WANT HAND!"

If his time as a lawyer and a clerk were formative, events years earlier turned out to be much more important for both Dworkin and the philosophy of law itself. As a Rhodes Scholar at Oxford in the late 1950s, one of his exam papers was read by H L A Hart. It was the start of the Hart–Dworkin debate, an ongoing battle that has had a huge place in the philosophy of law ever since. Hart was famous, among other things,

for advancing legal positivism: very roughly, the view that morals are not necessary for legal decision making. Judges simply apply rules. Dworkin argued then, as he argues now, that moral values have a necessary role in the interpretive activities of judges. According to some accounts, Hart read Dworkin's exam paper and said to a graduate student, "This is trouble." What, exactly, was the trouble?

"Sidney Morgenbesser, a wonderfully funny man at Columbia, once said that the problem with pragmatism is that it doesn't work. The problem with positivism is that it doesn't work. It doesn't work descriptively. It doesn't work normatively. It's nevertheless kept alive much more in Britain now than in other countries by a political fact. Many people think that it's very important to explain the difference between judges and elected politicians. One way to try and explain that is to say that when judges decide what the law is, they are not making political judgements. ⋙

They're looking in the books, they're finding out who said what. It's a real challenge if you give that up. Judges *obviously* make political decisions. But then it's much harder to explain to the public why they shouldn't be elected, why it's not critically undemocratic for them to have the power that they do."

"In the nineteenth century, positivism had major political appeal. Jeremy Bentham, who invented it, thought it was good for utilitarianism, because there ought to be a division of labour: parliament does the utility calculations, because they're much better placed to do so, and then judges just apply their results to particular cases. I'm not a historian, but I think that's probably how it happened."

"But the so-called debate between me and Hart is much more nuanced than people take it. It's not just two views. Hart changed over the years, as no doubt I have." How, I wonder, does the debate stand now? What does Dworkin think about positivism, after more than fifty years of reflection?

"This isn't anything that would be very popular with the people who call themselves positivists, but I think that I've got a much better defence of positivism than they do. It starts in the idea that a theory of law is an interpretative theory, that is, it tries to make the best of a particular kind of practice, and doing that requires a political theory."

"What makes a theory of law true? Not the way people talk. Luckily, we've gotten over that mistake. Not what the dictionary says. Not what a sociologist says. What makes a theory of law true is a political theory. I can construct a political theory that says that we have a much better community, a much more just and fair community, much more democratic, if judges just do

what they're told. That's how we organise things best. That's what democracy means. Where else can a legal theory come from other than a judgement like that? Maybe someone disagrees and says, 'I've got a different theory about how things work.' That's where the argument should be made. The debate between positivism and non-positivism should be a debate within political philosophy."

How, I wonder, are the values of political philosophy unified with other values, as Dworkin claims they must be? He distinguishes moral values, which have to do with right and wrong, from ethical values, which figure into thoughts about how we should live our lives. He argues that we have a responsibility to live well, and when I ask him where that comes from, I'm momentarily in danger of being cross-examined by Dworkin the lawyer.

"Tell me what 'comes from' means. I don't know what the expression means here. It's not a question of *coming from* someplace. Why do I say that? Suppose I had to argue that we have a responsibility to live well. I would point out that much of what you think, and the emotions and reactions you have, presupposes it. This is an interpretive argument. I'm saying you already believe that you have a responsibility to live well. And if you say to me, 'No I don't, and I'll give up everything else that's required for me to believe that,' then I have no way of talking you out of it, except to say that I'm right and you're wrong."

Is he saying that I have a commitment to live well because it's presupposed by the way I actually do live, the way I really act?

"No, that's not why you have the commitment, but I think you have it. That's pretty much a ground level ethical claim on my part. You might say, 'Well if you just believe I have the commitment, that's not much of a defence,' but that's getting us back in the trap of thinking that there's got to be some neutral standpoint from which I can prove it to you. There is no such standpoint. So instead of saying I can prove it to you from a neutral standpoint, I say you already think it."

"That's not to say that it's just a matter of what you think, that there's no real truth. There is a real truth. I've just told you what it is. Perhaps you disagree, and you think that what I think is wrong. But that doesn't mean we're both wrong. Some people say that if you think one thing about responsibility, and I think another, then it proves there's no right answer. But what you and I agree on is that there is a right answer. We disagree about what it is, but we agree there is a right answer. So if somebody takes the third position, and says there is no right answer, he needs his own defence for that position. He's got no more compelling argument than you have or I have."

The clouds do break a little when Dworkin talks about the value of living a life well. Some maintain that a life can't have meaning unless it leaves behind something valuable – a cure for cancer or a collection of sonnets, say. There's the worrying thought that even a life as wonderful as that can't mean all that much, particularly if you think that, in the fullness of time, there won't be anyone around to benefit from the cure or read the sonnets. Dworkin argues that these gloomy thoughts neglect a distinction between a life's product value and its value as performance.

"The product value of a life can be measured in different ways. Think of the Elizabethan carpenter who helped to build the Globe Theatre. Now, the product value of his life, how the world was different in virtue of how he lived, is enormous, but that doesn't show that he made a success of living. It's just to say the result of his having lived is good. The result of Fleming having lived the way he did was that we have penicillin, and it saved a lot of lives. That's also true of the cleaning woman who left the bread overnight so that mould grew on it."

"The only way to argue for any proposition about value is to make another claim about value"

"But we might say that a person lived his life in a more compelling way, a way that showed a better performance. Let's say a dancer dances brilliantly, and then there's nothing. That doesn't mean that something hasn't happened, but what happened is a matter of how a task was done."

I wonder if there's a conflict between various values here, whether there might be trouble for the hedgehog. On the one hand, Dworkin argues that how someone else lives ought to matter to me, and on the other, there's a person's dignity, his responsibility to make his own choices. But suppose someone has made some bad choices and is now in distress. I want to help, but he's chosen that life and that world. Isn't there a tension between wanting to help and respecting a person's choices? If I help, don't I step on his dignity?

"I don't know what tension you feel. There are two questions. One question is, has he made a mess of things? The answer is yes. Is there something which I have a responsibility to do for him? ⯈⯈⯈

Maybe yes, in spite of the fact that he's made a mess of his life." Is it just the fact of human suffering that creates this responsibility?

"There's a distinction between what we owe as individuals and politically what we owe. I do think we owe much less as individuals than we owe collectively. In politics, we owe other people equality, equal concern and an equal share of resources, but we've got to figure out what that

"Moral concepts are works in progress"

means. In my view that takes account of what choices people have made. If people have chosen not to work or not to invest or not to study, that limits what they're entitled to have."

"But what decent humanity requires is different. It's less, but it's not constrained by some notion about how wise they've been in the past. If you see someone lying in the street, whether you have a responsibility to help that person doesn't depend on why he's in the street. He's suffering, and you have to respond to that. But when it comes to some different question, for example, 'Should he get welfare?', then it might matter. That's a collective decision about what he's entitled to have. Now, if he's dying, even collectively we owe him something. But if he's simply not got as much as he would have had had he worked harder – he's a man who says, 'I don't really fancy work and I have nothing in my bank account so help me' – I don't think he's got a case."

There's another interesting thought about living well that figures into Dworkin's account of value: you can be wrong about whether or not you're living a good life. It's an objective matter.

Some people are perfectly happy and think they're living good lives, but they're wrong. How does one judge that another's life is not lived well?

"You only come to that conclusion if you have an idea of what a good life is and what a bad life is. Again we're always on the edge of the statement that, unless you can get outside your own judgements and prove it from a different direction, then it's only subjective. You think this, I think that, but there's no fact of the matter. That's why I wrote the first part of the book, to try and say all of that's a mistake. When we come to the question of whether someone is living well, we have to think about it and come to a conclusion."

"I think bankers, or anybody who has six billion dollars and wants to make that seven, and spends a lot of energy going from six billion to seven, is silly. They misunderstand what it is to live well. Now Fred Goodwin or somebody like that would say, 'I disagree. I think the essence of living well is going from ten billion to eleven billion.' Well, he's wrong and I'm right."

I ask Dworkin finally about how the moral and ethical propositions he's been pursuing support his claims about justice.

He says, "There has to be in my view a transition that explains what happens when we organise ourselves in a state, in a political community. The most striking thing that happens is that harming people becomes permissible. You are not allowed to drag me someplace, but if you're a policeman, you are allowed to hurt me. Now what explains what has happened in the transition? I think that the fact that coercion is permissible changes the game. We don't owe each other equality of treatment, as individuals, but when we're starting to hurt each other, and claim we are entitled to do that, then we owe each other much more.

Ask Ronald Dworkin anything

At **tpm online**, we invite readers to suggest questions for our interviews. To pose a question, visit blog.talkingphilosophy.com.

Here's a question from James P Houston. "Gauguin behaved badly in the 'moral' sense, neglecting obligations and responsibilities to his family for the sake of his art. Would you say that Gauguin was ethically right but morally wrong? Or if one can only remain ethically right while one is also morally right, does that mean Gauguin, having pursued his art at the expense of family and duty, failed to live well?"

Dworkin replies, "I make a distinction between having a good life and living well. I think that you shouldn't do what is wrong in order to have a better life. There's no doubt in my mind that Gauguin produced wonderful things, the product value of his life was very high. But if you ask the narrower question, 'Did he live well?', I think the answer is no."

"Many further questions arise. Are we glad that he made the choice he did? Is the world better in virtue of the choices he made? These are not the same as, 'Did he make the correct choice?'. I think that if we're interested in the idea that people owe self-respect, that they have a responsibility to live well, I think we have to bite the bullet and say that you should care more about whether you're compromising your dignity, whether you're treating yourself with the right attitude, than about the product value of a life. Many of your readers will point to Gauguin and say that's counter-intuitive. Then I think you need to move a bit forward in time. Not all the way to the explosion of the sun, but a while, when there are no more Gauguins because they're all dust, and then you say, 'Why is the kind of value that he produced in the paintings more valuable, if you accept what I say about performance?' Hard question. I'll have to say more about Gauguin."

Therefore we need a theory of justice, which is different from a theory of how we should treat each other decently, and that's what I try to develop."

We can, Dworkin thinks, be led by the same considerations to the conclusions that we must treat others with dignity, organise ourselves justly and live with self-respect – reflection in one domain supports reflection in another. He says, in his book's epilogue, that "Without dignity our lives are only blinks of duration. If we manage to lead a good life well, we create something more. We write a subscript to our mortality. We make our lives tiny diamonds in the cosmic sands." What, I wonder, is that "something more"?

"We create something more in the way in which, for certain people, a brilliant dance or a brilliant dive is something more. It doesn't last. But it occupies the time other than simply as duration. It creates something that has performance value. Now, this is all vulnerable to somebody who says, 'I can't see why that's value. It's all over. No dance. No value. I can't understand why something good has happened.' But if you do feel the tug of that, you can see what more is created."

As I put away my notes we talk a little about reviewers. Dworkin wonders whether his reviewers can be expected to read the whole of his book. If they haven't, he forgives them. It is, after all, 500 pages long. One who probably did read the whole book somehow ends up comparing Dworkin, in a way, to a hotel. "He said my life is like a hotel in which people talk to each other. If it had to be a hotel, he says, it would be the Savoy. Did you know that in fact the Savoy has been closed for a year?" There's a pause, then Dworkin starts laughing, and he barely gets the line out, "It desperately needed modernisation!"

Mathew Iredale
sci-phi

The shocking truth about consciousness and creativity

The theory behind creating artificial neural networks is quite simple. The brain is made up of millions upon millions of neurons that communicate with each other through physical connections known as synapses, the junction where one neuron connects to another. If one can replicate these neurons and their synaptic connections, then one can gain greater insight into how the brain works, and hence greater insight into that holy grail of neuroscience, consciousness. But recent research by Christof Koch, Costas Anastassiou and their colleagues at the California Institute of Technology has provided strong evidence that artificial neural networks leave out a key component of neuronal communication: their electric fields.

It has been known for some years that the brain is awash with electrical activity – not just from individual neurons communicating with each other, but from the countless overlapping electric fields generated by the neural circuits of these communicating neurons. Their existence can be measured externally as EEG waves and are particularly strong in specific brain regions,

such as the hippocampus, which is involved in memory formation, and the neocortex, the area where long-term memories are held.

With the exception of severe pathological conditions such as epileptic seizures, which induce very strong fields, these comparatively weak fields were thought to be a mere epiphenomenon, much like the sound of a heartbeat, which may give an indication of the state of health of the heart, but doesn't serve any physiological purpose. But it is now believed that these fields represent an additional form of neural communication. According to Anastassiou, while active neurons give rise to extracellular fields, the same fields feed back to the neurons and alter their behaviour (a phenomenon known as ephaptic coupling), even though such neurons are not physically connected through synapses.

It might be thought surprising that the impact of extracellular fields on surrounding neurons had not been investigated before, but the authors point out the severe difficulties in conducting an experiment on living cells in the absence of extracellular fields to observe what changes in neuronal behaviour when there are no fields to influence them. Their solution was to focus on strong but slowly oscillating fields, called local field potentials (LFP), that arise from neural circuits composed of just a few rat brain cells.

Everything you want to know about **Mathew Iredale** is available at www.mathewiredale.info

Measuring those fields and their effects required positioning a cluster of tiny electrodes within a volume equivalent to that of a single cell body at distances of less than 50 millionths of a metre from one another; the width of a human hair. In so doing they were able to achieve a level of spatial and temporal resolution not seen before in experiments on extracellular fields.

They were surprised to discover that even very weak extracellular fields can alter neural activity. Fields may exceed two to three volts per metre in strength in mammalian brains, but Koch and Anastassiou observed fields as weak as one volt per metre having a clear effect on the firing of individual neurons, and increasing the synchronicity with which groups of neurons fired. It seems likely that ephaptic coupling plays a significant role in neural communication, given that, as Koch says, "such field effects increase the synchrony with which neurons become active together. This, by itself, enhances the ability of these neurons to influence their target and is probably an important communication and computation strategy used by the brain."

One interesting question raised by their research is whether *external* electric fields will have similar effects on the brain. Anastassiou believes that they will. "Physics dictates that any external field will impact the neural membrane."

By a fascinating coincidence, this conclusion appears to be supported by a recent but unrelated study by Richard Chi and Allan Snyder of the University of Sydney. Chi and Snyder have used what is known as transcranial direct current stimulation (tDCS) to influence subjects' abilities to solve unfamiliar problems (tDCS involves applying a weak direct current to the scalp via two saline-soaked sponge electrodes).

Chi and Snyder are not specifically interested in ephaptic coupling but rather approached their research from the observation that people often find it difficult to "think outside the box". People are strongly "hypothesis driven"; once we have learned to solve problems by one method, we often have difficulties in generating solutions involving a different kind of insight. Realising that people with brain lesions are sometimes more resistant to this so-called "mental set effect" than those with unaffected brains, they wondered whether the mental set effect could be reduced by non-invasive brain stimulation.

They point to research that indicates that artistic talent, owing to a different way of perceiving the world, can sometimes emerge spontaneously in those with dominant (usually left) anterior temporal lobe dementia. The exact mechanism by which such spontaneity arises is uncertain, but one basic ⊳⊳⊳

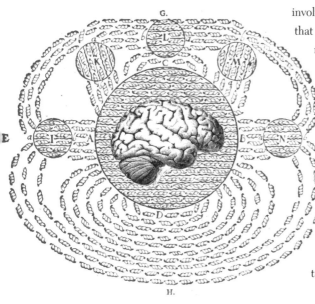

explanation is that brain dysfunctions, induced or caused by inhibiting and disinhibiting certain neural networks, may make our thought processes less hypothesis driven, thereby enabling access to a level of perception normally hidden from conscious awareness.

Chi and Snyder believe that this "raises a provocative possibility: can we facilitate insight problem solving in healthy people by *temporarily* inhibiting or disinhibiting certain areas of the brain?" To explore this possibility they used tDCS, "a safe, non-invasive technique that can increase or decrease cortical excitability and spontaneous neuronal firing in the stimulated region", on subjects who were asked to solve unfamiliar problems involving "matchstick arithmetic".

Participants were divided into two groups, only half of whom received tDCS (the other half were merely told they were receiving it). They were all asked to correct a series of false arithmetic statements, presented in Roman numerals constructed from matchsticks, by moving a matchstick from one position to another position without adding or discarding a stick. For example, the incorrect statement III = IX – I can be turned into the correct statement III = IV – I by moving one of the two matchsticks that make up the X to form a V. They were then asked to correct one false statement, VI = VI + VI, which requires changing a + sign to an = sign to form VI = VI = VI.

The authors used these two types of matchstick problem as previous research has shown that repeatedly solving problems requiring one kind of insight (changing an X to a V) impairs subsequent performance on problems requiring a different kind of insight (changing a + sign to an = sign). What the results of the research showed was that participants who received tDCS were three times more likely to solve the second type of matchstick problem than those in a control group. The electrical stimulation appears to have allowed the majority of the test group to "think outside the box" sufficiently well to enable them to solve the more difficult, unfamiliar problem in a way that the control group could not.

Chi and Snyder believe that they have achieved "the strongest cognitive enhancement we are aware of for a brain stimulation study", and the practical applications for such cognitive enhancement are clear. Most obviously, "brain stimulation might allow a person to examine a problem anew instead of through the mental templates of what is already known".

The exact nature of the role played by ephatic coupling in bringing about consciousness remains to be seen, and we are clearly some years away from being able to strap on an electric cap to provide us with the mental push needed to solve a particularly difficult and unfamiliar problem – if, indeed, this can ever be achieved. But what is clear is that our knowledge of that most complex organ, the brain, is not nearly as complete as we may have thought and that ideas once thought to be the preserve of science fiction (or the more esoteric end of philosophical thought experiments) may be closer to reality than we realised.

Suggested reading

"Ephaptic coupling of cortical neurons" by **Costas Anastassiou**, **Rodrigo Perin**, **Henry Markram** and **Christof Koch**, *Nature Neuroscience* 14 (Feb 2011).

"Facilitate Insight by Non-Invasive Brain Stimulation" by **Richard Chi** and **Allan Snyder**, *PLoS ONE* 6(2) (Feb 2011).

What, I believe, we need to cultivate in explorations of our own nature is the ability to resist being swept away from solid and clear ways of thinking into realms of fantasy, where more or less anything goes.

The animal you are

PAUL SNOWDON EXAMINES OUR INTUITIONS ABOUT MINDS, PERSONS AND ANIMALS

In his discussion of personal identity, written in the seventeenth century but still, probably, the first piece about the problem that students read, Locke is concerned to draw a distinction between what makes something the same man and what makes something the same person (or self). Locke summarises his theory of persons in the slogan "personal identity consists …. In the identity of consciousness". This is usually taken to mean that, according to him, a person's life stretches back only to periods the person can remember, as it is said, "from the inside". Locke is remarkably cagey about what the identity of a man consists in. This uncertainty derives from Locke's, commendable for his time, professed ignorance as to whether there are spirits (or souls), and if there are, how such entities are involved in human life. However, Locke is clear that whatever is involved in human identity, it is not a matter of consciousness. Locke's theory then seems committed to what has recently been called the man/person distinction.

According to him, as one might put it, where I, the person, am there is a man (or human), but the person (or self) is not the same thing as the man, since they have different conditions of persistence. A thing's "condition of persistence" is ▷▷▷

Paul Snowdon is Grote Professor of Mind and Logic at University College London. His forthcoming books include a collection of his own papers entitled *Essays on Perceptual Experience*, and, jointly edited with Stephen Blatti, *Essays on Animalism*. Both will be published by Oxford University Press in 2012.

Locke is remarkably cagey

what is required for that thing to remain in existence. For example, it is a condition for a house to remain in existence that the bricks making it up stay together and are not scattered over the ground. It is generally assumed that people as a sort have their own persistence conditions, and so have animals.

Locke's defence of the man/person distinction was so successful that philosophers simply took the contrast for granted, losing all interest in the notion of man or animal when discussing their own persistence conditions, and so representing any disagreement, to whatever extent, they had with Locke as disagreements about the concept of personal identity.

In what might be thought of as the recent classic period of discussion of personal identity, culminating in Parfit's brilliant *Reasons and Persons*, together with the ensuing debate about it, the notion of an animal (or man) is virtually invisible. Now, this invisibility ended in the 1980s when a number of philosophers were independently struck by how unsatisfactory this neglect is. This insight struck, among others, David Wiggins, Michael Ayers, Eric Olson and myself in Britain, and Peter van Inwagen and William Carter in the United States. We responded to this thought in different ways, given the contrasting metaphysical frameworks we worked within, but the idea of us as animals had returned to a debate from which it might be said Locke had removed it.

Having noted how central the idea of man (or the human animal) is to Locke's discussion, but how invisible it became in subsequent discussions

of personal identity, it needs to be asked whether Locke's conception of the relation between the person and the human animal is correct. The choice is between holding that the human animal (or man) is a distinct thing from the person, and holding that the animal and the person are the same thing. The view that, contrary to the long-standing Lockean framework, they are the same thing, is the view currently called "animalism". Before presenting some reasons that indicate, to varying degrees of strength, that adopting the distinctness thesis has real drawbacks, I want to

Animalism is an identity thesis

clarify animalism and the questions to which it is offered as an answer.

Animalism is an identity thesis; it says that a certain thing is the same as another thing. Now, normally when philosophers discuss the problem of personal identity they are searching for an informative specification of what is involved by way of links across time in the persistence of a person. So a typical (but I do not mean to imply plausible) candidate answer would be: a person P who does X at time t remains in existence so long as there is a person P* who can recall, from the inside, doing X at t. Clearly, the animalist identity thesis does not have that structure. It does not explicitly pick out links over time. However, it does so indirectly, because we have what we might call a shared proto-theory of animal persistence, and animalism implies an answer to the normal problem of personal identity by requiring that persons fall under and conform to that proto-theory.

Of course there are disagreements among animalists as to what the correct theory of animals is. But what seems clear is that even normally minded animals do not cease to exist if their mental capacities are destroyed, so long as they remain physically intact and alive. In such circumstances they remain in existence even though damaged. So the animalist identity thesis implies that any claim that the survival of people requires the presence of mental links over time is incorrect. It also seems clear that no one could think that some processes that purport to preserve mental links over time, without preserving that physically substantial thing which

is the animal, could seriously count as preserving the actual animal. The animalist should think, therefore, that simply generating mental links cannot be enough to ground real animal persistence, and hence not enough to preserve the persistence of the person as they think of the person. This explains how a thesis with the structure of animalism can imply substantial things about personal persistence.

A second clarification is needed. So far I have adopted a way of expressing animalism that regards it as saying that the person is the human animal. But if we are prepared to allow there might be entities that merit being described as persons who are not human – say God, or angels, or Martians, or robots, – then animalism should not rule them out. The content of animalism is better formulated as the claim that we, the persons hereabouts discussing these issues, are human animals. That is the nature that we have. Indeed, it is fairly clear, I suggest, that questions about the nature of persons as they interest us really are questions about the nature of ourselves. I have argued that we should understand animalism as a thesis about ourselves, rather than a thesis about persons in general, and also that, despite its form as an identity thesis, it has significant implications about the conditions of what is called personal identity.

The third clarification is that the animalist identity claim (we are identical to animals) should not be thought of as solely, or mainly, a thesis about what is known as "personal identity over time". One reason for not saying that it is a theory of personal identity full stop is that, as ▷▷▷

we have seen, animalists can disagree about the persistence conditions of animals. More importantly, we should think of animalism as a general, so to say, metaphysical characterisation of our nature, with myriad implications.

For example, if we are animals, it is also true to say that we are subjects of experience, and so it implies that there need be no more unity to the mind of a subject than there need be to the mind

In discussions of personal identity, the notion of an animal is virtually invisible

of an animal. On the face of it, an animal's mind can be radically disunified – imagine the sorts of surgical interventions that can break connections consistent with the animal remaining in existence and having experiences. So animalism also leads to a distinctive way of thinking about subjects and psychological unity.

Now I want to present some reasons that incline some of us to accept animalism. There is something artificial in dividing the reasons into those in favour and then subsequently considering those against. Part of the appeal of animalism, assuming it has an appeal, derives from a sense that the grounds that have convinced philosophers that animalism is hopeless are not as strong as their standard assessment supposes. However, in a preliminary presentation things simply have to be artificial. Now, I am assuming, as I hope any reader will allow me to, that where each reader of this article is, there is also a human animal. Animalism claims that the person reading and the animal (presumably also reading) are one and the same thing. Now, if the man/person

distinction is accepted it seems to follow that the same space is occupied simultaneously by two distinct things – the animal and the person.

This is sometimes called the thesis of the possibility of coincidence – the idea that two distinct things can coincide in the space they occupy. It is a thesis that strikes some as absurd. How can there be two things precisely coinciding in a single space (possibly, indeed, throughout their entire histories)? Now, if it is absurd then the conventional man/person distinction would have to be wrong, and there would be considerable pressure in favour of animalism. However, although this is a line of argument that has persuaded some, it rests on the conviction that coincidence is not a possibility, which is a conviction that is not obviously correct. So this reason strikes me as unreliable.

What is more striking, I believe, is that on any normal conception of them, there is a massive degree of similarity between the individual human animal and the individual person who occupy the same place. They seem to have the same spatial extension, the same parts, the same history (starting at the same point, and ending at the same point), the same causal roles – they seem to be the same in more or less every specific way. For example, if the animal is breathing then the person is breathing, and vice versa. Now, the most obvious explanation for this virtually exceptionless similarity is that the animal and the person are, in fact, the same thing.

The weakness of this argument, though, is obvious. Opponents of animalism hold that there are differences between the human animal and the person. What these are alleged to be I'll consider shortly, but they will reject the basic

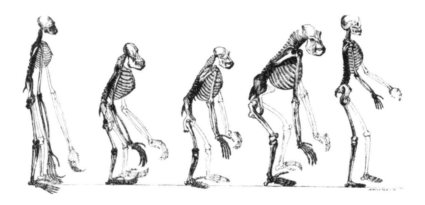

premise of the present argument. There is, according to them, no complete similarity, and so no explanation is needed. This reservation does mean that there is no proof here, but it can be suggested that a weaker conclusion looks plausible. Given the manifest extent of the similarity between person and animal, the animalist claim seems to be the view that counts as the default view. Discussion should start from it, and if we are not to accept it some strong reasons need to be provided. If that is correct the neglect of the view for quite a period must count as extremely regrettable.

A third reason or type of reason in favour of animalism is that there are difficulties in the idea of the man/person distinction. There are different ways to develop this idea, and here I shall sketch two closely related versions of the problem. The problem starts from the question whether the animal has mental states. It is obvious that the person or self does, but does the animal?

It surely seems quite clear that the human animal does have mental states, so initially I want to assume that is the correct answer to our question. Indeed, it is this conviction that fuels the appeal of animalism. What mental states does the animal have? It is hard to deny that the animal

itself has the same complex array of mental states that the person has. The human animal can think about itself, can talk, can reason, as well as have experiences and perform actions. If that is so then maintaining the man/person distinction seems to carry the implication that there are two subjects of experience and two mental lives being lived. Now, that is not a verdict that we accept as we start thinking about the nature of persons (or ourselves).

But the problem seems worse than this. On normal conceptions of what qualifies someone as a person, it is that they have (or are capable of having) the higher mental functions – such as self-consciousness and reason. These are the mental capacities that Locke cites in his famous and resonant elucidation of what persons are. But it seems that we have to credit these higher capacities to the human animal, in which case accepting the man/person distinction implies that there are two persons – as one might say, the non-animal person to be distinguished from the animal, and the personal animal. It would seem highly paradoxical to hold that there are two persons. We seem to have derived two paradoxical consequences from the man/person distinction. Clearly the opponents of animalism ▷▷▷

need to do some serious explaining at this point.

Here is a final line of thought. I have suggested that the question about the relation between the person and the animal can be viewed as a question about ourselves. How am I related to this animal? That is in effect what I want to know. We can get some purchase on the question if we can determine what "I" refers to, as used in that question.

Where each reader of this article is, there is also a human animal

Does it refer to the animal or not? But it seems to help with that question to ask how it comes about that there are "I" users in the first place. As we might say, the "I" in the crucial question refers to that thing, whatever it is, that "I" talk exists in order to refer to. But it would seem to be a plausible principle that such cognitive/linguistic devices have emerged in the course of evolution because they enable advanced animals to self-refer. We naturally think of such cognitive devices as akin to, say, other devices that natural selection has generated and preserved; they are preserved because they yield functions for animals that animals benefit from. This means that they are devices for self-reference by the animals that are lucky enough to possess them. In this way, reflections on the emergence of self-reference indicates that the subject of self-reference is the animal. Which is to say that it indicates that the animalist identity should be accepted.

This amounts, then, to a sketch of an argument from general biology to metaphysics. This may seem a surprising route to a metaphysical claim, but philosophers often appeal to considerations about language to support substantive (non-linguistic) conclusions, and in this case we are relying on empirical considerations about the origins of language, rather than brute semantic intuitions. Plainly, questions can be put to this line of thought, but it is not, I suggest, absurd.

There are then strong reasons in favour of animalism. However, I think that it is true to say that most philosophers do not accept it. Why? One way to think of the ground of opposition is to notice that animalism is an identity thesis. The person is the animal (where the person is). Now, an identity cannot be accepted if there is a (detectable) property difference between the two items. The ground for opposition is the general conviction that there are property differences between the person (or self) and the animal.

As we have seen there is a massive overlap or congruence of properties if we survey what we might think of as the ordinary features that our lives exhibit. But what philosophers have tended to think is that there are detectable differences in relation to what is possible for the person and for the animal. These differences come out when considering what might be called possible, even if not actual, dissociation cases. There are fundamentally two kinds of such cases. One sort of possible case is where we start with the person and the animal occupying the same space at the same time, but as the case develops the person is counted as ceasing to exist whereas the animal remains. One candidate for such a case would be where someone suffers a traumatic injury that makes them what we sometimes call a "human vegetable". There is life (perhaps artificially sustained), and so surely an animal, but no mental capacity. About such cases many judge that the person no longer exists.

Another type of example fitting this pattern that has been suggested is what used to be called cases of multiple personality disorder. As popularly conceived, in such occurrences there is associated with a certain human animal a definite personality, linked to a battery of memories and values, and a name to which they answer. After some time this psychological syndrome vanishes and is replaced in the same animal by a contrasting personality, set of memories and values, and self-professed new name. There is one animal but it is proposed that one person (or self) has been replaced by another. Cases

of this sort can be called [A and not P] cases – indicating that they are supposed to be examples where there is the same animal but not the same person.

But the sorts of cases that have had most influence on philosophers are ones that can be called [P and not A] cases. These purport to be cases where we start with a (coincident) person and animal but which develop in such a way that the person remains but the animal is no longer there. The example that has seemed most convincing is that of brain transplants. The standard example was first set out by Sydney Shoemaker. In his example we start with two people, Brown and Robinson. Both have their brains removed (for medical reasons) but, by mistake, Brown's brain

is returned to Robinson's body, and to avoid extra complications Robinson's brain perishes. It seems that we now have one person whom we can name Brownson. But is it Brown or is it Robinson?

Shoemaker suggests that the correct judgement is that Brownson is in fact Brown. Assuming that our psychological character is preserved in the brain, we can say that Brownson will

Brain transplants have seemed powerful anti-animalist cases

remember Brown's life, have Brown's character and beliefs, and Brown's values, and so on, and will be sure that he is Brown. This psychological similarity and continuity between Brown and Brownson, according to Shoemaker and most philosophers, makes it the case that Brownson is Brown. In which case we have the same person, but on the face of it Brown is no longer housed in or attached to the same human animal. So there is the same person but not the same animal. Now, there are, of course, other candidate [P and not A] examples – for example, head transplants – but brain transplants have seemed very powerful anti-animalist cases.

The initial anti-animalist argument derives then from the conviction, encouraged by reflection on such cases, that the person and the animal can "come apart". If so, they can hardly be the same thing.

If the arguments on both sides have struck you as powerful and plausible then we have to acknowledge that we have the task of evaluating them and also assembling, if we can find it, new

evidence to determine what the truth is about our relation to the animals where we are. I'll now raise some questions about the anti-animalist case that has been sketched. On the whole, in these anti-animalist examples, it is not really in doubt what the correct thing to say about the animal is. We feel confident that we can trace it in the developing story. The issue that is more unclear is what is happening to the person. What is it right to say about the person in such cases?

What of the [A and not P] examples? There is no general demonstration against the possibility of such cases, and so it is a matter of deciding what to say case by case. It helps, it seems to me, to consider such stories by imagining that they involve people who matter to you. So imagine your father suffers the accident. Would you seriously deny that he, your father, was himself still alive and in the hospital bed? When the hospital authorities ask you when you will be visiting your father would you really react by asking who they are talking about, since your father no longer exists? It seems to me you would not.

Next, imagine in the second example that it is your brother. Do you seriously have any inclination to think that your brother's whereabouts are unknown and that talking to you is a totally new person? Rather, we think of such abnormal psychological developments as illnesses that befall people. Our aim is to cure the people to whom they happen. More needs to be said, but despite their popularity in philosophical folklore such examples do not really seem like genuine [A and not P] cases. The [not P] description is implausible.

Such [A and not P] cases seem, on reflection, fairly weak because we have an established way of thinking of them according to which they really concern the same person, even if it is a way we tend to lose sight of when philosophising. With suggested [P and not A] cases the situation is different. We do not have an established way of thinking about them, since they do not occur. The fundamental question is whether opponents of animalism are right to be confident as to what is correct to say about such examples. Once we ask this, possible reasons for being less confident suggest themselves.

First, even if more or less everyone initially regards the person as going with the brain, it has to be acknowledged that the final verdict needs to be made in the light of all the evidence, and so it may be that some initial and quite strong convictions have to discarded. I have not investigated here lines of reply to the pro-animalist arguments – and that is a weakness in the overall strategy of argument here – but they also surely seem strong and convincing. So there is no entitlement to insist that the brain transplant intuition just has to be accepted.

Second, we can ask whether we are entitled to trust what I am calling our brain transplant intuitions. We can distinguish two broad conceptions of our conceptual practice of tracing ourselves over time. On one conception we do so in virtue of having an understanding of what our kind of persistence involves, an understanding that allows us to generate reliable verdicts about all sorts of imaginary cases. The second conception is that we are entities that are able to trace themselves in the world we find ourselves in, but that we must fix what the nature of our persistence is by investigating what kinds of things we in fact are tracing. Then, but only then, can we determine verdicts about such merely imaginable cases. This is a rough contrast, but people

who feel confident about what to say in brain transplant cases need to consider whether such confidence is based on a proper understanding of our conceptual practices.

Third, an alternative way of thinking about such cases can be proposed, and it may not be without merit. Organs can be transplanted. What was one animal's liver can become another animal's liver. Similarly, the organ of cognition (or

How can two things coincide in a single space?

mentation) that sustained cognition for one thing might be able to become the organ of cognition for another creature. On this way of thinking it is not that brain transplants transfer people; rather, a single organ for doing something goes from one person to another. Robinson may get a new brain, just as he can get a new liver. Philosophers who attach supreme importance to thought and cognition may find this an unnatural way of thinking, but that may not be how it does, and should, strike everyone.

I have been trying to put some question marks against some anti-animalist arguments. But it is obvious that these moves constitute merely the first moves in a complex debate, and in some respects I have not even sketched the first moves of the debate. What, I believe, we need to cultivate in explorations of our own nature and persistence conditions is the ability to resist being swept away from solid and clear ways of thinking into realms of fantasy, where more or less anything goes. But it is too early yet to say whether animalism is the view that avoids fantasy.

As Dr Johnson said, argument is like a crossbow: it owes its force to the mechanisms of the bow, as argument owes its force to its intrinsic rational power. But testimony is like the longbow: we cannot tell what it will do unless we know the strength of the user.

Telling stories

GREGORY CURRIE CONSIDERS FICTION AS A SOURCE OF KNOWLEDGE

Fictional stories are not naturally occurring objects. They have authors. To be understood, they must be read as the products of agents with certain intentions. But such stories also often have narrators – a person within the world of the story who knows about what is going on and tells us about it. And narrators in fiction often know a surprising amount about the people whose activities they describe. Authors, of course, see to it that they do, for otherwise there would not be much of a story. This creates opportunities and problems: Watson's daily amazement at Holmes's powers encourages us to be amazed; Fielding's narrator in *Tom Jones* (someone we have every encouragement to identify with Fielding himself) delights in telling us things no observing human could really know, while ironically declaring himself ignorant on various points; the narrator in Conrad's *Under Western Eyes*, a modest pedagogue and certainly no possessor of magical powers, tries with more seriousness to explain how he knows so much about the Russian revolutionists and refugees who pass through Geneva: "Wonder may be expressed at a man in the position of a teacher of languages knowing all this with such definiteness. A novelist says this and that of his personages, and if only he knows how to say it earnestly enough he may not be questioned upon the inventions of his brain ... Art is great! But I have no art."

But the explanation – the narrator heard it from someone else – does little to account for his intimate knowledge of such scarcely knowable things as Rasumov's mental turmoil as he tries desperately to justify the betrayal of the assassin Haldin. As so often, the issue is unresolved,

Gregory Currie is professor of philosophy at the University of Nottingham and author of *Narratives and Narrators: A Philosophy of Stories* (Oxford University Press, 2010)

and leaving it so might be taken to be the price of a good story, were it not for hints that this narrator is unreliable, a characteristic increasingly common in nineteenth-century literature and almost obligatory in the twentieth century. Taking the narrator's word for it might once have seemed to be part of the contract readers enter into with authors, but now the convention is to trust them only when no more interesting option is available.

Narrators, then, must sometimes justify their claims to know, and may at any time be suspected of passing on error rather than knowledge, sometimes deliberately. But all this concern with truth and truthfulness is just part of a game. We don't really wonder how Fielding's or Conrad's narrator could know these things, because in reality the author made it all up, including the narrator's relation to the whole. In these matters authors cannot be said to be reliable or unreliable, because they stipulate what happened in the story; they don't discover, or mis-discover it.

But don't authors sometimes tell us things: things they believe, or at least want us to believe? Conrad does say in the preface (speaking in his own voice, and from outside the fiction itself), that writing *Under Western Eyes* was "an attempt to render the psychology of Russia itself". It was a novel, he said, by which he hoped to "express imaginatively the general truth which underlies its action". In this, it seems, Conrad aimed at truth, so the question arises as to whether he arrived there.

And some people at least have thought Conrad successful

in this. Even if you are wary of the idea of a peculiarly Russian psychology, you might think that there are peculiarly Russian circumstances, and that Conrad did a fair job of describing how a real human mind might react to some of them. Certainly Conrad gives us a vivid picture of a brutal, desperately spiritual society, and the faddish, self- and other-deluding people who think they know how to redeem it.

Many learn more history from fiction than from textbooks

Is this powerful picture a true one? Perhaps that is setting the standard too high. Is it a picture with significant amounts of truth in it? A picture that is close to the truth (if that's a different thing)? Or does it, in the midst of failing to give a picture with any significant overall reliability, give us islands of important truth in a sea of falsehood?

I haven't done any surveys on this, but my guess is that many people would favour at least one of those options. And of course there is nothing special about Conrad. Faced with narratives of power and beauty from any quarter we get the strong impression that we are being treated to a glimpse of something importantly true. Our next remark, though, is always that these "truths" are hard to state.

How might fiction give us truth? Two models are worth looking at: the testimony model, and the thought-experiment model. Both can be illustrated from sources we would not immediately describe as ⧩⧩⧩

Joseph Conrad

fiction, but which do, we see on reflection, work by creating little fictional scenarios intended to instruct. Take testimony first. In Jesus's story of the prodigal son, the characters and events described are, we may assume, unreal, but there is a clear purpose of informing us of God's relation to human kind, and the role that free will plays in this relation. But the story is not self-

Can fictions be evidence for truth?

sustaining; Jesus vividly characterises a certain imagined interaction between humans, and what we understand to be the factual and moral import of the story depends on what we think Jesus intended that import to be: we take the story to be evidence for a certain reliable opinion that Jesus held and which he wants to convey to us. The story's power to educate us is the power of testimony.

Parables can seem a very indirect way of communicating information, more so novels like Conrad's; we think of testimony as working in much more direct ways, as when you want to tell me it's raining outside, and say "It's raining". In normal cases, it will be said, speakers who want to communicate something to us do so using words and sentences that actually mean what they want to communicate. And fictions, if they are meant to inform, usually do so in quite the opposite way: what the text describes is usually just the fictional events.

Perhaps the appearance of anomaly in calling fictions "testimony" arises because we hold a false view of how language works. One of the interesting features of Relevance Theory, originally devised by Dan Sperber and Deirdre Wilson, is that it challenges the assumption that there is a close relation between the words used and the testimony conveyed. On their view, words uttered rarely if ever coincide in meaning with what the speaker wants to communicate. Rather, words serve as bits of evidence for what the speaker means and words will often do that well even though they are distant in meaning from the speaker's meaning. Perhaps we can see parables and novels as merely further extending the distance between what language means and what speakers use language to communicate. That way we may speak with a good conscience of the testimony available in fiction.

On this view, fictions are bits of evidence that the writer believed something, and we have to decide whether to believe her. Can fictions sometimes be evidence of another kind – evidence for the truth of what is being claimed, rather than evidence that it is being claimed? Yes. Philosophers often exploit this possibility, telling us stories about runaway trains, violinists on life support systems and so on, which are designed to support or to undermine some philosophical theory. Generally, we are invited to make a judgement about the story concerned – that the case described is morally right or allowable, or possible or would, if certain things held, be bound to occur that way. Bernard Williams seeks to convince us of the possibility of moral dilemmas by constructing a case ("Jim and the Indians"), which, he hopes, strikes us as both possible and as constituting such a dilemma. We may agree with Williams or not, but in deliberating on whether this claim is right we need not give any weight to the fact

Illustration for *Don Quixote* by Gustave Doré

that Williams believes the claim; our purpose is to decide whether the case Williams describes really has the features he claims it has: that is, that it is a coherent instance of a moral dilemma. Williams gives us a fiction that serves as a thought experiment.

We might think that, of the two, the thought experiment model is the better, since testimony is a second-class source of knowledge. Not true. There is nothing wrong with taking testimony as a source of knowledge; we do that all the time and for good reason. People are often reliable sources of knowledge and we are generally alive to the signs of unreliability. On some topics we may need to credit the speaker with special powers in order to believe them, as with Jesus and the parable and, less dramatically, in

ordinary matters of value or specialist knowledge; I will not easily accept your opinion on the subject of personal beauty or how to stop global warming. That's why it is absurd, even by his own very generous standards, for Don Quixote to challenge the Toledo traders he meets on the road, insisting that they acknowledge the beauty of his imagined lady, Dulcinea, on his say-so alone and without seeing her or her picture.

Thought experiment is a kind of argument, although whether it is always reducible to the kind of argument we get with propositions related as premises and conclusion is a disputed matter. Testimony, by contrast, is not argument. As Dr Johnson said, argument is like a crossbow: it owes its force to the mechanisms of the bow, ▷▷▷

as argument owes its force to its intrinsic rational power. But testimony is like the longbow: we cannot tell what it will do unless we know the strength of the user. Judging testimony we judge the reliability of the testifier, not the intrinsic force of what is said.

Those who have thought that literature is a source of knowledge have not always been clear about whether they regard the educative power of fiction to derive from testimony or from argument (or, if they think both legitimate sources, what instances belong to which category). But there's a long tradition which comports with the testimony model, emphasising the wisdom of great authors ("Shakespeare was infinitely wise", said Thoreau). Of course we might think great authors wise *because* they are able to give us convincing and significant thought experiments. But my impression is that the wisdom of authors is sometimes presented as a reason for taking their testimony on important moral and psychological questions, and not as merely as something manifested in their arguments.

And on many subjects it is reasonable, or can be, to take testimony from the author of fiction. Many, I suppose, learn more history from fiction than from textbooks, assuming that while the characters in a historical fiction may be invented, or imagined words put in the mouths of real historical agents, the background to the events is reliably described, be it a Soviet labour camp, Revolutionary Paris or Nelson's navy. How sensitive should one be in these cases to the possibility that the author is unreliable?

" HOLMES GAVE ME A SKETCH OF THE EVENTS."

Sidney Paget, Strand Magazine

Perhaps it varies. Often one can depend on the author's reputation for reliability, or perhaps their lack of a reputation for error. We may also have a well-founded belief that the publishers would have done some checking themselves.

But it is one thing for an author to be celebrated for the rich texture of her historical background, and another for her to be fêted for what is often called "insight", the capacity to see more deeply into the human condition and to convey what she there discovers through her fictional portrayals. And in this kind of case, we might have more reason to question her reliability. The geography, dates and statistics of revolutionary France are reasonably well known and there are plenty of people who will call foul when an author gets them wrong. It's also easy to see how the author could come to know these very publicly available facts. What independent evidence do we have for the truth of the human condition? Are reviewers and critics to be relied on to check this? Their claims to expertise don't look any better based than those of the authors themselves. We could recruit professional psychologists to the task, but this does not seem ever to have happened in a systematic way. It's odd, surely, that people have confidence in the testimony of novelists on subjects one would normally treat as so complex and obscure that the speaker's credentials would be closely questioned and his claims scrupulously cross-checked, although we do none of those things. The reputation of certain authors as reliable testifiers to the human condition stands high, independently, it seems, of any real evidence in their favour.

Perhaps you find the testimony model unattractive. It seems, for one thing, to assign the reader a worryingly passive role in the generation of knowledge from fiction. If we take the way of thought experiments we might get a better result, for then we can think of readers as actively engaged to imagine the circumstances of the fiction in such a way that they can then see for themselves that the events described have some generally verisimilitude – or see for themselves that they don't.

This is a bigger topic than I can do justice to here. Let me make just a few negative points. First of all, the philosophical use of thought experiments is itself very much contested, as philosophers become sensitive to the idea that the intuitions these stories provoke may themselves be highly unreliable. Second, philosophers are usually careful to make clear what general thesis is up for discussion in the light of the thought experiment. Novelists and playwrights, on the other hand, are heavily censured for "didacticism" if they do the same thing, so their audience is immediately at the disadvantage that they have to guess what ideas to consider. In practice, we may end up with no more than a swirling mass of vaguely formed ideas to think about, on which we may very well make little progress once we put down the book or leave the theatre. It's easy to imagine that we have learned something from an emotionally charged narrative, especially when attending to its language has costs us some effort.

I don't say there is nothing to be learned

We are strangely complacent in assuming we learn from fiction

from fiction. I do say we have been strangely complacent in assuming that we do learn, without any better evidence than our own feelings of having learned something. A school system that tested its effectiveness by simply asking the pupils whether they thought they had learned something would, I suppose, be written off as romantic folly. People who declare the arts important for (among other things) the enlightenment and insight they provide might consider this point.

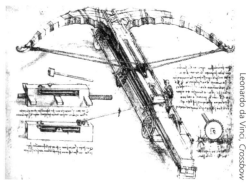

Leonardo da Vinci, *Crossbow*

letter from ...

Israel

SAUL SMILANSKY ON FORTUNATE MISFORTUNE

Both heaven and hell, a Jewish story says, are to be found in studying the Torah (scriptures): for the righteous, such study is heaven, for the unrighteous, hell.

There is much that we can take from this wonderful thought. One is the ideal according to which learning is paramount; a second, that matters do not really depend on one's surroundings, but rather it is the spirit of the study itself that forms the quality of one's life. Following in this path would be difficult, but inspiring. It certainly has its attractions in the Israeli setting, where difficult and occasionally dangerous situations threaten to interrupt philosophical work, raise thoughts about the urgency of the need to become more socially and politically involved, and even supply a ready excuse if one's philosophical attainments fall short. Such competing ideals of "pure" immersion in philosophical study versus social involvement trouble many local philosophers, and we shall visit this theme further.

Who was the first Israeli philosopher? We cannot claim to know, but surely a good contender

Saul Smilansky is professor of philosophy at the University of Haifa, and his most recent book is *10 Moral Paradoxes* (Blackwell, 2007)

is the prophet Nathan, who is less prominent than some of his colleagues such as Isaiah or Jeremiah, but he is my personal favourite. Arguably he can lay a claim to have discovered universal morality and human rights.

To recall the outline of the biblical story, King David lusted after the beautiful Bathsheba, who was, alas, another man's wife. He thus arranged that her husband, Uriah, be sent to the front, where he conveniently died in battle. Nathan severely criticises the king, targeting David with a thought experiment. Nathan asks David to tell him what he thinks about the following case, which involves a wealthy man, who owns many sheep. When this man has a guest, rather than taking a sheep from his own flock and using it in order to prepare the welcoming feast, he takes the sheep of another, poor man. This poor man is movingly described as having only one sheep, a ewe lamb, with which he shares his meagre supply of food. David is outraged at such an abuse of power and gross injustice, and declares that the offender must die. He thereby falls into Nathan's trap, for Nathan then tells him that he is that man. It is apparent how very similar was David's behaviour to that of the manifestly immoral, wealthy sheep owner.

I find this an amazing story, in a number of ways. Uriah is in fact not a Hebrew but a Hittite,

Francesco Salviati, *Bathseba begibt sich zu David*

David and Bathsheba

the story is amazing for other reasons: first for its very occurrence, and then for its being told to us, uncensored. David ruled over ancient Israel some 3,000 years ago. Even today, in dozens of undemocratic countries, one would be strongly ill advised to admonish the local ruler. Moreover, David was on the winning side of history, the triumphant leader uniting the tribes of Israel and establishing Jerusalem as the capital; one whose offspring were to be divinely blessed. Yet we are told in no uncertain terms of his grave faults, here as in other matters. The freedom then prevailing in ancient Israel, both to criticise and to report such criticism, is remarkable for its time, and would be the envy of a large proportion of the world's human inhabitants even today. Jewish civilization was, together with that of ancient Greece, one of the two sources of Western civilisation, through the Roman and Christian mediation. While in many areas the Greek influence was more important, the Jewish contribution was central in forming our understanding of morality.

Following the destruction of Jewish national independence by the Romans about 1,000 years later, around the time of Jesus, and then the occupation, in turn, by the Byzantine, Arab, Crusader, Mamluk, and Ottoman empires, there was very little philosophy going on here until the twentieth century. Some limited exceptions can be found with some interesting Greek philosophers in the Hellenistic period, with a few Church fathers, and in the various spiritual and philosophical schools associated with the Kabala, which flourished in the Galilee around the sixteenth century. In the twelfth century, Maimonides came up from Egypt and is buried in Tiberias, but his work was done elsewhere.

yet morality and justice nevertheless apply to him just as much. He is also a common man yet, again, he nevertheless has firm moral standing. We have here a striking illustration of the force of practical reasoning, equality, human dignity, and justice. Morality is universal, it is above power and privilege, and applies equally to ordinary foreigners and to kings. But beyond the content,

The modern Zionist movement emerged in the second half of the nineteenth century as part of the resurgence of European nationalism. It had a strong moral and philosophical impetus from the start. While there was a desire to regain political sovereignty and solve the practical "Jewish problem", and premonitions of the dangers facing Jewish existence in Europe, no less important was the quest for spiritual rebirth

Moral paradox is a part of daily life here

in the ancient homeland. A prominent thinker was Asher Ginsberg (known by his pen name Achad Ha'am) who believed that the highest priority was to establish a spiritual centre for the Jewish people. Socialist thinkers had egalitarian visions, culminating in the establishment of the first kibbutzim (radically egalitarian cooperative communities) at the beginning of the twentieth century; while the major contribution of more bourgeoisie intellectuals was the miraculous re-birth of Hebrew as a living language. A number of philosophers, including Martin Buber and Shmuel Hugo Bergman (Franz Kafka's close friend from Prague and a translator of Kant into Hebrew together with Nathan Rotenstreich),

were instrumental in the founding and early leadership of the Hebrew University of Jerusalem; where philosophy was taught from the start. The cornerstone was laid in 1918, and the university opened in 1925, a generation before the establishment of the State of Israel in 1948.

Gradually other universities joined Jerusalem, yet the country is small, and so is the philosophical community. I will limit my discussion to "general" philosophy rather than to Jewish philosophy, which is taught in separate departments. Today there are five universities in Israel, with medium sized philosophy departments (the Hebrew University in Jerusalem; Tel-Aviv University; the University of Haifa in the north; Bar-Ilan, a religious university near Tel-Aviv; and Ben-Gurion University in Beersheba, in the south). In addition there is a small contingent of philosophers in the Open University (modelled after the British one), and some philosophers in smaller colleges, as well as in other departments (particularly those of political science, law, literature, Judaism, Arabic and Far-Eastern studies).

Israeli philosophers have made significant contributions to various fields, contributions that I could not hope to list here. Just to give one example, in the history and philosophy of science, we find widely respected figures such as the late

Berthold Werner, panorama of Haifa

The David B. Keidan Collection of Digital Images from the Central Zionist Archive

Martin Buber

the pressing needs of the armed forces over the years. Such "fortunate misfortune" and indeed moral paradox is a part of daily life here.

Philosophers in Israel have an exceptional record of social and political involvement, mostly but not exclusively on the left. Yael Tamir who taught in the philosophy department at Tel-Aviv was the education minister (representing Labour) a few years ago; and the current finance minister in the Likud-led coalition, Yuval Steinitz, was a member of my own department at Haifa, before moving to politics. Even more important is the continuous informal engagement of philosophers in public life. Philosophers played a major role in the establishment of the Israeli "Peace Now" movement in the 1970s, as well as other protest movements and human rights organizations. Quite a few philosophy lecturers (as well as students) have refused to serve in the army or in the West Bank, some serving prison sentences as a result. The army's code of ethics, first devised by the philosopher Asa Kasher in the 1990s, was later re-written (putting it in line with the prevailing ethical and legal norms of warfare), and again the role of philosophers was paramount. This involved a lengthy and intensive process of applied philosophical thinking by a task force in which I was privileged to participate, together with the philosophers Moshe Halbertal, Avi Sagi and Daniel Statman. Philosophers also regularly sit on national committees, such as the "medical basket" standing committee, which determines anew every year the priorities of public funding of various medicines and medical services.

It is noteworthy that there is a widespread public interest in philosophy in Israel. Philosophical books often sell well, and there is a substantial body of translations, predominantly ⊳⊳⊳

logician Yehoshua Bar-Hillel and historian of ideas Amos Funkenstein; the death last year of the philosopher of physics Itamar Pitowsky deprived us of one of our most distinguished contemporary philosophers. In more recent years it seems that the balance of interest of many has shifted towards moral philosophy and adjacent fields. This builds upon Israel's unfortunate "natural advantages" – I can recall, for example, at least four papers by Israeli philosophers in the past decade, in the top journal *Ethics* alone, on topics of warfare and terrorism. This will perhaps come to parallel the story with high-tech: Israel is considered the most innovative high-tech place outside of Silicon Valley (chances are that the chips of your computer and the algorithms of your Google searches were developed in Israel); this success is attributed in large measure to

made up of the classics and contemporary continental literature (there is, alas, far less analytic philosophy available). There is also continuous popular demand for various not-for-credit series of talks, combining philosophy with fields such as literature, film and science. And hundreds of students, both Jews and Arabs, choose to go on and pursue graduate work in philosophy, while a surprising number of them (many older students,

Philosophers in Israel have a record of political involvement

for example) can have little hope of extrinsic gain, and are studying philosophy for its own sake. With all this in mind, it is perhaps unfortunate that philosophy is taught in Israeli high schools only sporadically.

Yet with all this lively and pluralistic engagement, the daily life of Israeli academic philosophers largely resembles that of philosophers in other Western countries, with similar worries about administrative meddling and under-appreciation, budget cuts, declining undergraduate enrolment in the humanities, and the limited ability to offer tenure-track positions to young graduates. The generational shifts have considerably reduced the earlier continental (mostly German) and historical orientation, and four of the five major departments are noticeably inclining in an analytic direction. Only Tel-Aviv firmly resists the Anglo-Saxon domination; many of its members specialise in various strands of continental philosophy, and some even cultivate French postmodernist tendencies.

While many Israeli philosophers have studied in the country, it is common to go abroad for this purpose, and many and possibly most of the leading philosophers received their PhDs from top universities in North America and Great Britain. Recruitment and selection processes, which were far from ideal in the past, have gradually become more open and rigorous. While the language of teaching is typically Hebrew, there is a strong requirement to publish abroad, mostly in English, for tenure and advancement. The regular salaries are far from outstanding, but generous sabbatical leave and travel budgets allow close contact with the wider philosophical community, as well as a welcome escape from the local tensions. Judging by the record of publication, the quality of professional Israeli philosophy has probably never been as high and, given that the external dangers can be contained (one scarcely dares to hope for peace), and that there are not too many further budget cuts, there is reason to be cautiously optimistic. One hopes that Israeli philosophers will aim to meet the ideal of "pure" philosophical study at the highest level, while not forgetting the example of Nathan.

© MathKnight

The problem with mercenaries can't simply be that they do what they do for money. It would be pretty hypocritical to condemn them for providing combat services for money, given that we generally honour and praise those members of our nation's Armed Forces who fight at the front line – even though they receive a pay cheque at the end of every month.

Are mercenaries just warriors?

DEANE-PETER BAKER ON THE MORALITY OF GUNS FOR HIRE

In its most recent annual session, the United Nations Human Rights Council (UNHRC) passed resolution A/HRC/15/L.31, which addresses "The use of mercenaries as a means of violating human rights and impeding the exercise of the right of peoples to self-determination". In the resolution, the UNHRC declares itself, among other things, to be "*Extremely alarmed and concerned* about recent mercenary activities in developing countries in various parts of the world, in particular in areas of conflict, and the threat they pose to the integrity and respect of the constitutional order of the affected countries".

When as august and influential a body as the UNHRC expresses itself to be "extremely alarmed and concerned", presumably this should make us sit up and take notice. Perhaps, indeed, it should cause us to have the occasional sleepless night. I confess, however, that reading the Council's resolution (let's just call it

"the mercenary resolution") did not fill me with anxiety and disquiet. Instead, I found it more than a little puzzling.

Consider first the title of the mercenary resolution. It's directed against "The use of mercenaries as a means of violating human rights and impeding the exercise of the right of peoples to self-determination". That certainly sounds like something to be concerned about. After all, violating human rights and the self-determination of peoples is undoubtedly a bad thing. But, on reflection, it seems somewhat odd for the resolution to be focused on *mercenaries*. To see why this is so, consider another, ⊗⊗⊗

Deane-Peter Baker is assistant professor of philosophy in the department of leadership, ethics and law at the US Naval Academy and author of *Just Warriors, Inc.* (Continuum, 2011). This is the author's opinion not that of the US Naval Academy.

fictional, UNHRC resolution directed against "The use of boxcutters as a means of hijacking passenger aircraft in order to crash them into buildings and commit mass murder and violate state sovereignty." If I were to read the title of such a UNHRC resolution my first instinct would undoubtedly be that this is something I'd want to support. But then it would be very odd indeed if the resolution turned out to be all about the evils of *boxcutters*. That would seem to miss the point, to say the least.

Perhaps, however, we might imagine from its title that the point of the mercenary resolution is to delineate inappropriate uses of merce-nary forces (violating human rights, impeding peoples' self-determination) from legitimate uses of mercenaries. If that were so, then focusing the resolution on mercenaries would make some sense. It turns out, however, that this is not the case. As we read on further we find the UNHRC expressing itself to be "*Convinced* that,

notwithstanding the way in which mercenaries or mercenary-related activities are used or the form they take to acquire a semblance of legitimacy, they are a threat to peace, security and the self-determination of peoples and an obstacle to the enjoyment of human rights by peoples." So, then, *no matter* how they are used and *no matter* what form they take, mercenaries are nonetheless a threat to peace, security, the self-determination of peoples, and human rights.

Seriously? Imagine how odd an analogous claim would be if it appeared as part of our imaginary "boxcutter resolution": "Convinced that, notwithstanding the way in which boxcut-ters or boxcutter-related activities (what could this possibly *mean*?) are used or the form they take to acquire a semblance of legitimacy, they are a threat to airline passengers and crew, office workers, bystanders and state sovereignty." Such a statement is patently absurd in the case of boxcutters, so why does the UNHRC think

© Chmee2/wikicommons

© Chmee2/wikicommons

the apparently equivalent statement about mercenaries is not absurd?

Perhaps the answer lies in some intrinsic difference between the nature of mercenaries and the nature of boxcutters. After all, it might be argued, boxcutters are mere tools, with no particular propensity to either a good or evil use of their cutting abilities. Mercenaries, on the other hand (so we can imagine the argument continuing), have some intrinsic propensity to be used for evil, making the mercenary more like a dedicated torture device, such as an iron maiden, than a boxcutter.

Following this logic, the idea must be that this intrinsic propensity to be used for evil makes it entirely sensible to consider mercenaries to be threatening no matter what they're actually used for or what controls are in place regulating their use. (I take it that the latter is what the mercenary resolution is getting at when it refers to "the form they take to acquire a semblance of legitimacy", although the meaning of the phrase is certainly not clear.) To flip to the iron maiden analogy, perhaps it might indeed make some kind of sense to think of the iron maiden as being threatening *even if* its owner only ever used it as a somewhat inefficient although entertaining tool for making orange juice at parties, and *even if* it were kept under lock and key and only ever brought out and used under the close scrutiny of an officer of the law. Perhaps, although frankly I don't find myself breaking into a sweat at the very thought of that scenario. But even if we grant that

some things can be threatening regardless of how they are used or controlled, does it really make sense to think of mercenaries as being more like iron maidens than boxcutters?

One reason to think that mercenaries are not like iron maidens is that, while it's pretty easy to see what's morally problematic about the nature of iron maidens – they're designed solely for the purpose of committing acts of torture – it turns

The UN is "extremely alarmed about mercenary activities"

out to be rather difficult to pin down the moral "badness" that's generally assumed to be inherent in mercenaries, or even to work out what, exactly, a mercenary is.

What, for example, is the morally odious feature that places the "mercenaries" of the Flying Tigers of the Second World War (American airmen under contract to the Chinese government who fought against Japanese imperialism prior ▷▷▷ to the United States's entry into the war) in the same category as Bob Denard, the notorious French soldier-for-hire who roamed Africa for three decades, and whose activities included four attempts to overthrow the government of the Comoros? Or, for that matter, what common feature entitles the UNHRC to also heap blanket condemnation on the "private companies

© Chmee2/wikicommons

offering military assistance, consultancy and other military and security-related services on the international market" that the mercenary report also deems to fall into the morally abhorrent category of "mercenary"?

While space limitations prevent me from offering a full analysis here, it doesn't take all that much head-scratching to realise that there

Are mercenaries more like iron maidens or boxcutters?

are no good definitions of the word "mercenary" that both capture the moral badness that is presumed to be inherent in that term and is also a good fit to the characteristics displayed by all those that the UNHRC and others would like to paint with this particular brush. The problem with mercenaries can't simply be that they do what they do for money – most people do the jobs they do at least in part for that pay cheque at the end of the month, and they don't thereby earn moral excoriation. Nor can the problem be that mercenaries engage in combat operations for money. For one thing, most of those that the UNHRC would like to call mercenaries simply don't do combat operations. They provide advice and training, they supply and service equipment, they provide logistical support and the like, and a small minority use guns to guard things in dangerous places (rather like the numerous security guards who guard things in South Africa, the dangerous place I hail from). But even if there were private contractors providing genuine combat services (as, say Executive Outcomes did

in the 1990s under contract to the governments of Angola and Sierra Leone), it would be pretty hypocritical to condemn them for doing so for money, given that we generally honour and praise those members of our nation's armed forces who fight at the front line – even though they receive a pay cheque at the end of every month. True, we would certainly consider someone who would do *anything* for money, and who valued money above all else, to have gone over to the moral dark side. Adrian Walsh and Tony Lynch of the University of New England in Australia have coined the delightful term "lucrepath" to describe such a person. But it's pretty obvious that only a small portion, at best, of those that the UNHRC seeks to tarnish with the label "mercenary" are actually lucrepaths, and that those inflicted with lucrepathology are to be found in all walks of life, not merely among the ranks of the mercenary hordes that the UNHRC seems so concerned about.

It is, of course, undeniable that (to use a more morally neutral term) some contracted combatants have been involved in morally questionable activities. But this is an unfortunate, but probably inescapable, feature of the existence and use of military forces in general. Far, far, more atrocities and coups have been carried out by national military forces than have been carried out by contracted combatants. Once one recognises that contracted combatants employed by states stand in

© Chmee2/wikicommons

© Chmee2/wikicommons

essentially the same fundamental relationship to those states as do the states' national military forces – both groups are *agents* of the state – it becomes increasingly difficult to draw a neat moral line between them. This point explains the (I hope excusable) pun in the title of my book *Just Warriors, Inc*. My claim is not that all contracted combatants are just in the moral sense – that would be obviously absurd – but rather that they are "just" (merely) combatants, and what defines whether or not they are just (moral) warriors are essentially the same features that define whether or not the soldiers, sailors, airmen or marines of a nation's armed forces are (morally) just. Some uniformed personnel fail this test, as do some contracted combatants. But the opposite is also true: some military personnel are worthy of honour and respect, and there are no good reasons to believe that the same could not be true of some contracted combatants.

The UNHRC, it seems to me, would be far better served by focusing less on "the menace posed by the activities of mercenaries" and instead focusing its attention on the states or non-state groups that employ contracted combatants – or militia forces, or bandits, or secret police, or soldiers, or whomever – to violate human rights or impede the exercise of the right of peoples to self-determination. Contracted combatants, like their uniformed colleagues, are (as a category at least) more like boxcutters than iron maidens. They can be used for good or for harm. What matters then, is who uses them, and for what purpose.

Happy Birthday, David Hume

The mighty David Hume was born on 7 May 1711. Enthusiasts might find an excuse to raise a glass twice, because before Parliament's reform of the calendar in 1752, Hume's date of birth was 26 April. Whatever your calendrical preference, join us now in marking Hume's 300th birthday with a celebration of his legacy.

Hume has been called Le Bon David, The Terrible David, Saint David, the greatest empiricist, a most fiendish sceptic, the best philosopher to write in English, an indecent atheist, a sophist, a genius, and on and on. Don't worry about what he was. The question we've asked our contributors is this: what is he to us now?

In this forum we'll discover why Hume is so many things to so many people, and see how it is that he continues to inspire us today. We'll also consider the influence that Hume has had on our understanding of causation, the place of emotion in moral reflection, and the idea that there is an enduring self. Given the recent resurgence in thoughts about God and design in nature, there's much in Hume's treatment of religion that's relevant today, and we take this up too.

We begin with Barry Stroud's thoughts on Hume himself. It's worth peering back through the centuries in the hope of catching a glimpse of Hume the man. Hume, not just his philosophy, is worth celebrating too.

It is for Hume's sympathetic attention to the complexity of human nature, and for his trying to do justice to it at the deepest levels of philosophical reflection, that we should honour his memory.

A perfectly wise and virtuous man

BARRY STROUD ON HUME'S LIFE AND CHARACTER

t is good to take notice of significant anniversaries of the great figures of the past. They don't need it; their positions are secure. But it is good for us to understand and acknowledge their contributions to everything that makes our life the way it is now. It keeps us connected with the richness of the culture we all live in, whether we know it or not.

David Hume is certainly one of the great men of our culture. He was born in Scotland in 1711, in a century filled with greatness. Adam Smith, Thomas Reid, Robertson, Diderot, d'Holbach, Rousseau, Voltaire, Johnson, Boswell, Smollett, Garrick, Goldsmith, Reynolds, Gainsborough and Haydn were all close to him in age. His older contemporaries Newton, Hutcheson, Butler and others had inspired Hume as a youth, just as Kant and Gibbon, younger than Hume, drew inspiration of different kinds from what they found in his work.

Hume conceived, wrote, and published his masterpiece, *A Treatise of Human Nature*, and spent several years waiting in vain for anyone to notice it, all before the age of thirty. By forty he had been rejected on ecclesiastical grounds as professor of moral philosophy at the University of Edinburgh, but was the leading moral philosopher of the kingdom, writing graceful essays on philosophical, political, economic and more popular subjects. By fifty he had produced his monumental six-volume *History of England*, the most popular and best-selling history ever published in Britain, until supplanted on that pinnacle by the work of his great admirer Gibbon. Hume's was a new and more "philosophical" kind of history, describing events involving strong passions and allegiances from a more detached and dispassionate point of view, with the attitude of an observer of human nature. That meant that ⋙

Barry Stroud is Willis S and Marion Slusser Professor of Philosophy at UC Berkeley. His book *Hume* (Routledge, 1977) won the Matchette prize.

members of almost every politically engaged faction found the book biased or complacent or (the most general verdict) merely Tory.

Hume left for posthumous publication a work that remains as important and as urgent today as when it was first written: *Dialogues Concerning Natural Religion*. It should be (but, alas, is not) read by anyone who even thinks of inferring from the remarkable order and arrangement of the observable world as we know it the presence of an intelligent design of a concerned creator of the universe.

Hume's basic and most powerful philosophical ideas are very much alive in one form or another in philosophy today; certainly in all philosophy that is conducted primarily in English. Those influential ideas do not, of course, belong to or derive from Hume alone. They are part of a long philosophical tradition from which he shaped and developed in new ways problems and ideas he had inherited and had seen the real force of. To say those ideas are alive today is not necessarily to say they are widely accepted in the form in which he defended them. That is not the best way to measure the value and influence of philosophical ideas. Hume's work is alive in current philosophical controversy, in its effects on the way philosophical problems are now formulated, and on what is thought to be the range of acceptable solutions to them. He presented in detail one of the first and clearest, and also one of the most provocative, descriptions of what it would be like to understand human beings and every aspect of human life as part of observable nature. It was something that had not been seriously tried before.

He saw, and stressed, as few philosophers before him had done, the rich variety and complexity of human motivation and aspiration, all of which must be understood by any adequate "science of human nature". He agreed with tradition that "man is a reasonable being". But "man is a sociable, no less than a reasonable being", he wrote; and "Man is also an active being", and "requires some relaxation".

"It seems, then, that nature has pointed out a mixed kind of life as most suitable to the human race, and secretly admonished them to allow none of these biases to *draw* too much, so as to incapacitate them for other occupations and entertainments …. Be a philosopher; but, amidst all your philosophy, be still a man."

It is for Hume's sympathetic attention to the complexity of human nature, and for his trying to do justice to it at the deepest levels of philosophical reflection, that we should honour his memory. He was a great philosopher who made lasting contributions to a subject fundamental to the understanding of human life. But for all his philosophical greatness, he was also, as a philosopher, a great man, an admirable human being. And for this too he should be honoured today, as he was at the time of his death.

His lifelong friend Adam Smith wrote in retrospect not only of Hume's writings and achievements, which he admired above all others, but of Hume's "temper [which] … seemed more happily balanced than that perhaps of any other man I have ever known … that gaiety of temper, so agreeable in society, … was in him certainly attended with the most severe application, the most extensive learning, the greatest depth of thought, and a capacity in every respect the most comprehensive. Upon the whole, I have always considered him, both in his lifetime and since his death, as approaching as nearly to the idea of a perfectly wise and virtuous man, as perhaps the nature of human frailty will permit."

He is the darling of naturalism or the bogeyman of scepticism, a friend to virtue or an unwitting party to incipient nihilism. He is politically conservative, or a liberator from old views. He is a fideist, an advocate of faith over reason, or a precursor of Richard Dawkins.

Hume's living legacy

P J E KAIL ON WHY HUME IS MANY THINGS TO MANY THINKERS

The weighty figure of David Hume, 300 years after his birth, remains a formidable presence in philosophy. Publishers' catalogues announce new books on aspects of his philosophy in every new edition, and a society in his name publishes a journal devoted to every aspect of his thought. There are "Hume's laws", "Hume's principles" and "Humean positions" in moral philosophy, philosophy of mathematics, and metaphysics. He is still a reference point for aesthetics, economics, political philosophy and for countless other areas of intellectual endeavour. Few university students in philosophy graduate without studying some Hume. His personality remains too. Pictures of him adorn many a philosophy office wall, and he has been the subject of plays and

television drama. On Ebay one can find David Hume badges, fridge magnets and other such trinkets. Why, and in what senses, is Hume such an abiding figure?

Hume is, speaking tenselessly, many things to many people. He is the darling of naturalism or the bogeyman of scepticism, a friend to virtue or an unwitting party to incipient nihilism. He is politically conservative, or a liberator from old views. He is a fideist, an advocate of faith over reason, or a precursor of Richard Dawkins. He boldly offers an austere metaphysics or counsels ⮞⮞⮞

P J E Kail is university lecturer in the history of modern philosophy at St Peter's College, Oxford, and author of *Projection and Realism in Hume's Philosophy* (Clarendon Press, 2007)

humility in the face of a world unintelligible to us. He is an object of interest for figures as diverse as Gilles Deleuze, Edmund Husserl, A J Ayer and Immanuel Kant. He is the greatest philosopher to have written in the English language or, according to Elizabeth Anscombe, a "mere sophist", albeit a "brilliant" one.

The fact that Hume admits of many readings, provokes such a variety of reactions and excites

On Ebay one can find Hume fridge magnets

the interest of thinkers with vastly different philosophical orientations is at least as significant, and perhaps more so, than what Hume "really meant". These multifaceted views of his achievements, often apparently, and sometimes really, inconsistent with one another, do not simply reflect the humdrum fact that philosophical views can be misperceived. Of course it is true that there are some fairly gross misperceptions about his thought, reflecting perhaps a lack of engagement, ignorance, prejudice or a combination of these factors. A case in point is the mistaken view that Hume defines miracles out of existence. But that is true for any philosopher. And again it is true, for any philosopher, that there can be subtle misinterpretations, although ones that can mistake what a given thinker's fundamental conclusions are. Historians of philosophy exert a great deal of energy trying to understand the views of

philosopher when taken in the context of their own problems and their time, and this is an important philosophical activity in its own right.

However, there can be subtle misinterpretations that have themselves a very lasting impact and significance, and if Hume the man might not have meant as much, Hume the text was important in their invention, in that they do much to afford and support such readings. One such misinterpretation is the view that Hume is a sceptic about "induction", holding that we have no reason at all to think that what we have observed in the past gives us any reasons for beliefs about the future. The practice of inferring how things will be in the future from how they have been in the past is as reasonable as using tea leaves to predict the results of the World Cup. Although there are dissenters, Hume scholarship tends to view this as a mistaken reading of Hume's intentions and conclusions. Nevertheless, this "Hume" still makes his annual visit to introductory philosophy classes, and it is undeniable

that this misinterpretation is hugely influential on philosophy. As an aside, I was first drawn to philosophy precisely because of the "problem of induction", as were, I subsequently learned, a number of very prominent Hume scholars, all of whom now believe that this is not at all what he intended.

A second subtle but extremely significant misinterpretation is the idea that Hume advocated something known as the "Humean theory of motivation": very roughly the idea that beliefs alone do not motivate actions. Instead, motivation must involve both a belief and a separate desire. Such a view, central to metaethics, is occasioned by Hume's discussion in "Of the influencing motives of the will" in his *Treatise*, where he famously says that reason is, and ought only ever to be, the slave of the passions. Because readers looking at these claims with some historical distance assumed that by "reason" Hume meant "belief" and by "passion" he meant "desire", a whole complex and valuable literature was born. However, the assumptions about what he meant by "reason" and "passion", and thus the interpretation built upon them, is somewhat questionable in the light of recent scholarship.

That two important aspects of Hume's legacy are probably misinterpretations does not in any way detract from his importance if we rightly distinguish what he himself thought and what lines of thought his text can inspire. That, again, is something that is true of other philosophers. But of course there are more things to Hume, and some of them rarely found in other thinkers. One such thing, as David Pears once said, is that Hume makes for excellent philosophical

company. The word "company" is exceedingly appropriate. His writings often evoke a sense of engagement with a real person, a certain intimacy seldom found in philosophy. I suspect this partly explains why some commentators appear to have a jealous regard for their own interpretations of his philosophy. He appears to speak to us because his writing is stylish, ironic, brilliantly argumentative and sharp. He is playful and provocative, and

How Hume is read is as important as what he really said

engages or enrages depending on one's temper. But of course Hume is not all style over content (although style must not be forgotten). He wrote on a vast number of topics central to philosophy, and in ways that embody different, and sometimes not obviously consistent, approaches. These approaches mix, in varying degrees, the psychological, phenomenological, metaphysical, naturalistic, genealogical, analytical and sceptical. Because his thought is so rich and varied, it embodies insights, approaches, and arguments that speak to many different concerns.

One can react to these riches in different ways. John Passmore's *Hume's Intentions*, published in the 1950s, saw many such approaches in Hume and doubted whether they could be made consistent. Many years earlier, L A Selby-Bigge wrote that Hume's "pages, especially those of the Treatise, are so full of matter, he says so many different things in so many different ways and different connexions, and with so much indifference to what he has said before, that it is very hard to say positively that he taught, or did not teach, this or that particular doctrine … This makes it ⋙

easy to find all philosophies in Hume, or, by setting up one statement against another, none at all." Such views are exaggerated, and scholars claim that Hume is far more consistent than Passmore or Selby-Bigge might make him seem. I think that's right, but mere consistency among trivial or uninteresting strands of thought does not make for greatness. The point is rather that the aspects of his thought, be they consistent or not, are by themselves inspiring, even if they inspire a "no". And when considering Hume's legacy, one should bear in mind the elementary observation that particular aspects of this richness take on a greater or lesser saliency depending on the context and interests of his readership. This is partly because philosophical topics come and go, sometimes to return, but, on a deeper level, the overall meaning and significance of Hume's general philosophical stance can vary dramatically depending on the prevailing intellectual climate. A sketch of his changing role in philosophy reveals this fact.

Kant, so the legend goes, developed his critical philosophy as a reaction to a Hume whose main thrust was sceptical, and Kant's view of Hume would eventually return to Great Britain in the guise of T H Green's idealist-leaning critical study of Hume. Green's Hume embodies what is wrong in empiricism, and opens a door to scepticism that can only be shut by Hegel. In Scotland, Hume was seen in his lifetime, and well into the nineteenth century, as a (sometimes affable) anti-hero, an advocate of an extreme scepticism, but one linked inextricably to irreligion. It is only a slight exaggeration to say that many Scottish philosophy professors thought they had a duty to refute Mr Hume. That he was such a target partly owed itself to Hume's fame rather than the intrinsic character of his philosophy, although this is not to say he was always understood in caricatured fashion. His apparent equanimity at the time of his death was the subject of much discussion long after its fact, and for some it was exemplary of the possibility of virtuous atheism (although Hume himself rejected the label "atheist"). Hume's attitude to the world – his "philosophy" in the broadest sense of the term – was perceived as a mixture of good sense, wit, brilliance, learning and benevolence, free from anxious terrors of the unknown or the comforting promise of riches to come. This was a threat for some and an inspiration for others. The way in which the manner of his death is painted as something important for philosophy is surpassed only by Plato's portrait of the death of Socrates. It is worth noting, furthermore, that the importance of Hume's role as a virtuous atheist is not merely a thing of the past. In Italy, the moral philosophy of Eugenio Lecacaldano, Italy's leading atheist, is a direct consequence of his reading Hume, and finds popular expression in his book *An Ethics without God*. He also is instrumental in promoting the study of Hume in Italy, helping to produce reliable editions of Hume's works in the 1970s.

Whatever forces led to the more secular approach of "analytic" philosophy in the twentieth century and the revolt from the perceived excesses of Hegelian idealism, the change in culture meant that Hume could occupy more positions than that of a sceptical and irreligious anti-hero (or just plain hero). One factor in this is the seemingly straightforward character of some of his prose. Many years earlier, Arthur Schopenhauer, educated in England and feeling oppressed by German philosophy, remarked that there is "more to be learned from each page of David Hume than from the collected works of Hegel, Herbart and Schleiermacher taken together". Furthermore, the *Enquiry Concerning Human Understanding* and the *Treatise* seemed to have a (literally) no-nonsense approach to the limits of our knowledge and the progress of science. What we can understand, and what we can express in language, must be appropriately related to sensory experience, otherwise it is mere "sophistry and illusion" and to be "committed to the flames", as Hume writes near the end of the *Enquiry Concerning Human Understanding*.

From these views, Hume argues that there is no self that is the owner of experience, no powers and forces underlying regularities, and talk about physical objects must somehow translate into statements about the passing flow of experience. Sceptical worries disappear as mere misinterpretations of our language, and the world shrinks to fit our mind. The sceptical Hume takes at least a back seat, while Hume the slayer of metaphysics and the advocate of science is at the wheel. The complex psychology of the *Treatise* and the sceptical moments are

Two important aspects of Hume's legacy are misinterpretations

of course recognised, but not viewed as part of Hume's "real achievement". Indeed, his brilliant insights into the true method of scientific philosophy are marred by confusing psychology with philosophy, or failing to think his insights through. By contrast, for Karl Popper, Hume's scepticism remained, but rather than threatening religion, it threatened the practice of empirical science. Popper, who took the methodology of science to be central to philosophy, saw Hume as setting the "problem of induction" and failing to solve it. Hume is philosophy of science, his writing on moral philosophy largely ignored.

Aspects of Hume's texts are certainly amenable to these readings, and, as I said at the beginning, how Hume is read is as important as what he really said. But the two attitudes of the previous paragraph cannot be said to have emerged from a serious attempt to understand Hume on his own terms. The sceptical reading of T H Green did, however, provoke an attempt to so ⧸⧸⧸

understand him. This was Norman Kemp Smith's reading of Hume as a *naturalist*, a reading first offered in a two-part article published in *Mind* in 1905 and then expanded upon in his enormous book *The Philosophy of David Hume*. The Hume presented there is a far more complex and ambiguous figure, whose aim is neither to advocate sceptical conclusions, nor offer a reductive metaphysic or champion Newtownian science (as

Aspects of his thought are inspiring, even if they inspire a "no"

many were already doing when Hume wrote), but instead to offer a new theory of human nature. Human beings are part of the natural world, and so they and the issues that have plagued philosophy are to be treated by the science of human nature. The scepticism is in the aid of Hume's naturalistic agenda, and not his resting place. The naturalistic ambitions of Hume became the focus of another classic study, this time Barry Stroud's 1977 *Hume*, a work that sees Hume's abiding significance in precisely his advocacy of naturalism. But Stroud is no apologist for naturalism and sees Hume's philosophy embodying its problems as much as its spirit.

It is fair to say that when Hume's name is invoked in contemporary philosophy his scepticism still takes a back seat. The naturalistic impulses in his works are lauded (or taken again to be an example of mistaken philosophy). His moral philosophy is seen as humane and grounded in worldly existence, although his critics see it as insufficient to account for the demands of morality. The Hume that figures in contemporary metaphysics, while austere, is not sceptical. He holds that causation consists in regularities and the world comprises distinct existences that have no necessary connections (a view I might add that I think is not Hume's, but I am in the minority and in any case the fiction is an important one). The metaphysician then constructs the richer world from this "Humean mosaic", or shows how thoughts about something richer (morality or causation for example) are the result of the mind projecting itself onto the world. Philosophy of religion is catching up with Hume too, and not just in the sense that the arguments in natural religion he criticised many years ago continue to be refined and refuted. Hume's lesser known work *The Natural History of Religion* has taken on a new saliency as the philosophical significance of investigations into religious belief becomes the focus of greater attention in works like Daniel Dennett's *Breaking the Spell: Religion as a Natural Phenomenon*. The sometimes hostile reception of Dennett's work recapitulates the hostility that met Hume's *Natural History*, and, I think, reveals the critical edge of this form of naturalistic approach to religious belief.

Hume's legacy is a living one. Philosophers will continue to be inspired by attitudes, arguments, theses and methods in his engaging and brilliant works, and Hume scholars will continue to debate, and sometimes squabble over, what he really means. Naturalism is in the ascendancy and Hume is there. If philosophy were to take a transcendental turn, Hume would still be there (there have always been readings of Hume that turn him into Kant). Who knows where Hume and philosophy will go next?

As time moves on, both our philosophical language and our conceptual frameworks evolve, since they are highly abstract and not closely tethered to the relatively solid ground of ordinary life. So to understand Hume's thinking, it becomes necessary to "translate" what he says into categories increasingly different from his own.

Finding inspiration in Hume

PETER MILLICAN EXPLAINS WHY WE CAN LEARN FROM PHILOSOPHY'S PAST

Why, as we pass his 300th birthday, do we still study David Hume's philosophy? He wrote copiously on many things, including economics, politics, psychology, religion and, especially, history. Yet few historians – either students or academics – now read his monumental *History of England*, and even fewer economists pay any attention to Hume (or even to Adam Smith, who built on his close friend's theories to become the greatest founding father of the subject). Psychology, again, is a mature experimental science, with little concern for speculations from centuries ago. So why do philosophers continue to study Hume so intently? Are they just dinosaurs whose lack of progress condemns them to rehashing forever the same old stuff? And as for specialist historians of philosophy, wouldn't their time be better spent on more neglected authors? Haven't Hume's works been adequately worked over dozens (if not hundreds) of times, making any further "novel interpretations" a pointless exercise in philosophical imagination? If Hume could write clearly, then surely by now we must know what he said? And if he couldn't, then why is he accorded such respect?

Peter Millican is Gilbert Ryle Fellow and reader in early modern philosophy at Hertford College, Oxford, and Illumni David Hume Fellow at Edinburgh University. He has published widely on Hume, edited *Hume Studies* from 2005 to 2010, and developed www.davidhume.org

These sceptical doubts about the history of philosophy must occur to many observers of the academic scene, and they deserve to be taken seriously. By way of response, note first that philosophy almost by definition focuses on difficult questions, whose methods of solution – let alone the answers suggested – are typically debatable and conceptually unclear. Thus at the time he wrote them, Hume's explorations in psychology and economics came under the heading of "moral philosophy", the philosophy of the human world. He was breaking new ground, developing concepts and methods that would be built on by later generations of thinkers. But once these later thinkers had established new disciplines on those foundations, most future work in psychology and economics ceased to count as part of "philosophy". Thus the questions that we continue to call "philosophical" are typically those that have not yet been solved, and whose very method of solution is open to live debate.

It is important to recognise, then, that progress by philosophers does not necessarily register as progress in philosophy. And in fact many of the great developments that created the modern world were driven by philosophers, most obviously in the political and religious arena (Locke, Rousseau, Voltaire, etc.), but also in the physical sciences (through Bacon, Descartes, Leibniz and other "natural philosophers"). Even among this impressive company, Hume can claim as high a place as any, his position enduringly secure both as "philosopher" and as seminal pioneer of the "science of man", which since his time has grown hugely in many of the directions that he was the first to advocate and explore. All well and good, you might say – we can agree that Hume himself was no dinosaur – but why does this give us any reason to study him now, other than from historical interest? Surely psychologists who want to understand the human mind have no need to study Hume's works, or to fight again the battles that he helped to win for them. They will instead follow the spirit of his philosophy, relying on the empirical investigation that he himself so ardently insisted was the only route to knowledge of the world (or of ourselves).

In many areas of psychology, all this is true enough, but there are other areas – particularly in the vicinity of the new multi-disciplinary field known as cognitive science – where things are far less straightforward, and where thinking through Hume's problems, in his way, can open our minds to new ideas that could prove genuinely fruitful. Thus Jerry Fodor has recently found inspiration in Hume's theory of ideas and faculties, writing a book called *Hume Variations* that argues: "Hume is remarkably perceptive about the components and structure that a theory of mind requires. Careful study of the *Treatise* helps us to see what's amiss with much twentieth-century philosophy of mind, and get on the right track."

But how can it be that going back to a philosopher of the eighteenth century can be useful for inspiring new thoughts (even within a field that didn't exist in his day)? This is the key point that needs to be explained in order to understand why the history of philosophy remains valuable to contemporary philosophers to an extent that is unparalleled within the historical study of other disciplines.

We have already noted that philosophy is focused on controversial and conceptually difficult areas, and it follows that those questions remaining within its scope (and not exported to the special sciences it spawns) commonly provoke strong advocacy and debate, while lacking the sort of empirical anchoring that would dampen the influence of prevailing currents of thought. So philosophy is highly subject to trends and fashions, and when a fashion is in full swing, it is all too easy to forget earlier ideas that are out of tune with it, even if those ideas were previously accepted as established truth. But fashion can bring benefits as well as costs. The confidence and group interactions that come from being part of a bandwagon can push things forwards with an energy that would otherwise be difficult to harness, and progress tends to be much faster if, for a time at least, inhibiting quibbles and sceptical worries are quietly ignored.

One relatively crude example of a philosophical fashion, probably fostered by the widespread influence of economic thinking today, is the tendency to see humans as overwhelmingly governed in their behaviour by rational calculation of self-interest. On this cynical view, a woman who volunteers to nurse a victim of an earthquake, say, is doing it only as a means to make herself feel better. Hume (like Adam Smith) rightly considers this picture of human nature ridiculous, appealing to the earlier arguments of Joseph Butler to highlight its fundamental flaw: "It has been prov'd [by Butler] that even the Passions, commonly esteem'd selfish, carry the Mind beyond Self, directly to the Object; that tho' the Satisfaction of these Passions gives us Enjoyment, yet the Prospect of this Enjoyment is not the Cause of the Passion, but on the contrary the Passion is antecedent to the Enjoyment, and without the former, the latter could never possibly exist."

Those who account for human behaviour exclusively in terms of a desire for personal pleasure are putting the cart before the horse. It might be that the nurse gets pleasure from the recovery of her patient, but if so, that is clearly because she first desires his recovery. The fulfilled desire is what generates the pleasure, and to suppose the reverse is to adopt a manifestly ridiculous model of human motivation: of a self-interested nurse who, although she has not the slightest concern for the patient himself,

Progress by philosophers isn't necessarily progress in philosophy

somehow inexplicably gains pleasure from his recovery, anticipates doing so, and plans accordingly. This picture of humans as constantly calculating rather than directly desiring outcomes is also implausibly rationalistic, as Hume observes with a characteristic move of his own: "Animals are found susceptible of kindness, both to their own species and to ours; nor is there, in this case, the least suspicion of disguise or artifice. Shall we account for all their sentiments too, from refined deductions of self-interest? Or if we admit a disinterested benevolence in the inferior species, by what rule of analogy can we refuse it in the superior?"

Plenty of people, both before Darwin and since, have espoused theories of human nature that would take us out of the natural world into some theoretical wonderland. Hume continues to provide a valuable (and beautifully written) corrective, and we need not be surprised to learn that Darwin was reading Hume on "The Reason of Animals" (in the first *Enquiry*) at the ⧉⧉⧉

time when he devised his theory of evolution by natural selection.

Thus the writings of classic philosophers can usefully remind us of worthwhile views and arguments that might otherwise be lost in the flow of fashion. In the specific case we have just considered, perhaps, the same could be achieved without reference to Butler and Hume, by simply cataloguing – in textbooks or encyclopaedia articles – their key observations and arguments that show crude "psychological egoism" to be a hopeless theory of human motivation. But quite apart from the aesthetic and cultural loss involved in this unhistorical approach, it will fail with philosophical trends that are relatively subtle and less specific, and which involve the application of common ideas, themes, and techniques to a wide range of complex and conceptually tricky issues. Here the value of older currents of thought can be fully maintained only if they are kept alive through active engagement, rather than merely recorded as positions frozen in time. And it is in this spirit that Fodor (as we saw earlier) comes to Hume, finding in him a champion for conceptual atomism against the dominant pragmatism and holism of Wittgenstein, Quine and others.

This need for active engagement is crucial to explaining why the history of philosophy is so distant from being an antiquarian study of past thinking. As time moves on, both our philosophical language and our conceptual frameworks evolve, since they are highly abstract and not closely tethered to the relatively solid ground of ordinary life. So to understand Hume's thinking, it becomes necessary to "translate" what he says into

categories increasingly different from his own. Making sense of his talk of mental faculties (e.g. "reason" and "the imagination"), for instance, requires careful interpretation, because he shares Locke's scepticism about faculty language, and yet several of his most central arguments (e.g. on induction, the external world, and the basis of morality) are couched in those terms. In struggling to understand what he means, we have to think things through in our own minds, informed as these may be by knowledge of recent philosophy and cognitive science. So even if we aspire only to follow Hume's own engagement with the problems – let alone to build further on his thoughts – we have little choice but to attempt such "translation".

It follows from this that interpretations of Hume will, quite legitimately, vary over time, and not only because scholars learn more about Hume himself. Even when our understanding of Hume has indeed moved forward, high quality older work (such as H H Price's 1940 book on

Hume's theory of the external world) can retain a distinctive value precisely because it views him through spectacles tinted with the fashions of the time, giving later readers an appreciation of unfamiliar aspects of his thought. Inevitably, interpreters will focus on elements of Hume's philosophy – including themes and subtle textures within it – that harmonise or are made vivid by their own particular context. Thus when atomism has been in fashion, scholars have recognised more easily (and been accordingly inspired by) the aspects of the *Treatise* that chime with that; when naturalism became all the rage, a different set of connections began to be appreciated that might previously have been entirely overlooked. This again shows how the coming and going of trends in philosophy, although incompatible with the steady, forward progress commonly expected in the sciences, can also bring complementary advantages.

To expect such steady progress across the board would anyway be unrealistic: given the nature of philosophical questions, it is humanly impossible to foresee, or even to recognise, all of the connections that might prove fruitful in the future, and often one has to "think oneself into" a position intensively and over time before one becomes able to envisage most of its range of possibilities. So trends and fashions are indeed to be expected, but notice here how an enduring focus on the texts of the "great, dead, philosophers", so far from rooting us immovably in the world of those classic thinkers, can play a quite different positive role. Without my interest in Hume, I might never have read Price's views on perception and "sense data". Through his book, the greatest philosopher of the eighteenth century has thus provided a connecting thread

through which the insights of a different period – the early twentieth century – can be conveyed forward even to those who have no special interest in that period. Thus one can learn greatly both about Hume and about philosophy through seeing his issues explored in a variety of ways, both over time and through the involvement of a variety of scholars with different emphases (and, of course, disagreements). This also facilitates

Darwin was reading Hume when he devised his theory of evolution

serendipity, the way in which interesting ideas can turn up unexpectedly, and chance observations or associations can prompt fruitful enquiries (perhaps quite distinct from the intentions of the relevant texts). One famous example is Einstein's recollection of studying Hume's *Treatise* "with eagerness and admiration shortly before finding relativity theory". Einstein did not approach Hume's text as a scholar, but his understanding of its "positivism ... was of great influence" and even "suggested relativity theory". Such serendipity can occur with all sorts of reading, but a particular virtue of going back to classical texts is that doing so forces us systematically to reinterpret our own ideas in their terms (or vice versa), providing an especially fertile source of novel connections

What makes all this so fruitful is the enduring richness of Hume's thought, which is generally so logical, insightful and wide-ranging that engaging with it deeply can provide valuable lessons and new inspiration to each succeeding generation. ⫸⫸

Philosophers as diverse as John Mackie (attacking religion and moral objectivism), Peter Strawson (on free will and scepticism), David Lewis (with his "Humean mosaic"), Annette Baier (interpreting reason as social and passionate), and Simon Blackburn (proposing a "quasi-realist" account of morality and much else) have found fertile seeds in Hume's philosophy. Nor does one have to be a "Humean" to learn from him, because even when he makes mistakes – and he makes a fair number – these are typically illuminating, and one can learn as much philosophically here, from teasing out exactly where the error lies, as one can elsewhere, from following his limpid prose through convincing arguments that invite no objection and harbour no hidden difficulties. Thinkers of Hume's quality are rare, and this is why historically minded philosophers tend to focus so much on the established canonical figures of the past rather than spending their time scouring libraries for forgotten heroes.

The first-hand philosophical engagement that is essential to grappling with Hume's ideas also explains why there will always remain room for multiple "interpretations", arising from our attempts to think his thoughts in slightly different ways, against different backgrounds, and with different emphases. Moreover when his text appears ambiguous or indeterminate, or leaves logical gaps, or merely provokes objections, scholars will have different preferences for how these issues are best to be resolved (e.g. over what line of thought provides the most faithful development of the Humean position). But this variety should not be seen as an invitation to relativism, or a sceptical denial that there is any interpretative progress to be had. Hume scholarship, especially over the past thirty years, has

moved forwards immensely from the simplistic caricature and distortion that marred so much earlier work, in which his friends (e.g. the logical positivists) enthusiastically recognised their own views in his canonical texts, while his foes (e.g. Christians) sought to ridicule his unpalatable principles. A tradition of sympathetic but careful and objective scholarship has now built up, facilitated by the availability of searchable electronic texts, and I fully expect that, over time, our understanding of Hume will focus and deepen, with many older interpretations being decisively refuted while the live options are progressively refined. In some cases, we will be able to establish solid conclusions about what Hume thought; in others, we will at least achieve a clearer appreciation of the range of positions that are compatible with his texts. As we gain this deeper understanding, I am sure that new insights will emerge, to benefit our own future philosophising as well as our appreciation of the past.

To sum up, active engagement in the history of philosophy keeps a rich variety of frameworks alive and under development, often seeking out imaginative ways of combining the old with the new. It can also provide a more balanced perspective on current orthodoxies, for those who might otherwise be carried along by the hubris of the crowd to dismiss alternative approaches, conveniently forgetting the long history of discarded enthusiasms. Secure building for the future requires learning from the past, and the history of philosophical fashion demonstrates very clearly the folly of putting all one's eggs into the currently popular baskets. Indeed, in the long term, it is very much in the interest of those now at the vanguard, that future generations of philosophers should take their history seriously!

Many philosophers came to regard "causation" as an illegitimate pseudo-concept. This was a dominant view in analytic philosophy until quite late in the twentieth century. Russell famously quipped that "the law of causality" was "a relic of a bygone age, surviving, like the monarchy, only because it is erroneously supposed to do no harm".

Hume's impact on causation

HELEN BEEBEE TRACES HIS EFFECTS

H ume's account of causation has a good claim to being one of the most influential views in the history of philosophy. It not only set much of the agenda for large swathes of analytic philosophy in the twentieth century and beyond, but it also awoke Immanuel Kant from his "dogmatic slumber" – as he put it in his *Prolegomena to any Future Metaphysics* – and prompted him to write the mighty *Critique of Pure Reason*, itself a hugely influential work and arguably the starting-point for the continental tradition in philosophy.

So why has Hume's view on causation proved to be so influential? Well, let's start with the state of play in philosophy at the time Hume was writing. The dominant view of causation at the time was a part of what Edward Craig (in *The Mind of God and the Works of Man* calls the "Image of God doctrine". The idea here is, as the name suggests, that we are made in God's image: our mental faculties are of course rather feeble compared to God's, but they are of the same *kind* as God's. If you were in the grip of the Image of God doctrine, you might think something like this. Our mental faculties are at their most perfect – their most God-like – when we're engaged in *a priori* reasoning, for example when we're constructing a mathematical proof. And in a mathematical proof, we can (if we're really good at maths) just "see" or "intuit" that each ⋙

Helen Beebee is professor of philosophy at the University of Birmingham and author of *Hume on Causation* (Routledge, 2006)

successive stage of the proof follows from, or is entailed by, the preceding stage. So, if our mental faculties generally are God-like, then the same kind of thing must be going on when we turn our attention to the causal structure of the world. At least in principle, if I look at some event – the cue ball hitting the black ball in snooker, say – I can tell, just by observing that event, what *must* happen next: I can infer, on the basis of just that

Van Inwagen called "cause" that "horrible little word"

experience, what the collision will cause, just as I can in principle tell just by looking at a mathematical theorem what follows from it.

Hume's fundamental insight when it comes to causation is that that story cannot possibly be right. No matter how hard I look, and no matter how much I know about the size and shape and weight of the balls and their position on the table, *nothing whatsoever* follows about what the collision is going to cause. Of course, what I *expect* to happen is that the black ball will move off in a certain direction and (let's suppose) land in the corner pocket. But that is not

something I can *deduce* just from careful observation of the collision. As Hume puts it: "If we reason *a priori*, any thing may appear able to produce anything."

A crucial – and perhaps the most influential – part of Hume's argument is that we cannot observe the causal relation itself. When I look at the snooker table, all I *see* is the cue ball hitting the black ball, followed by the black ball moving off: I don't see any "necessary connection" between the two. Because I have frequently seen this conjunction of events before, I come to *expect* the black ball to move – but this expectation is generated not by any kind of *a priori* inference. Rather, it is generated by "habit or custom": we are endowed with a kind of instinct that prompts us to expect, on the basis of past "constant conjunctions", that the same thing will happen this time. It is this insight – coupled with the empiricist thought that all of our "ideas" or concepts must be based on experience – that led analytic philosophers to go in one of two directions.

First, many philosophers in the empiricist tradition (itself traceable to the three great "British Empiricists", of whom Hume was the third, after Locke and Berkeley) came to regard "causation" as an illegitimate pseudo-concept. Since we cannot trace our idea of causation to

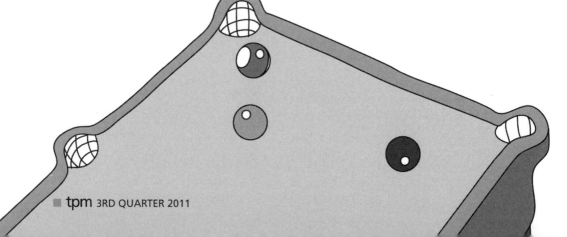

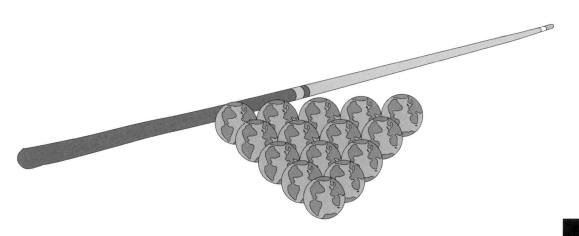

some observable feature of reality, we really don't mean anything at all when we say that one thing caused something else. Thus we should shun causal talk all together. This was a dominant view in analytic philosophy until quite late in the twentieth century. Russell famously quipped that "the law of causality" was "a relic of a bygone age, surviving, like the monarchy, only because it is erroneously supposed to do no harm", and Peter van Inwagen said of "cause" that it is a "horrible little word".

Second, some philosophers took the view that causation just *is* a matter of constant conjunction: all we mean when we say "the short circuit caused the fire" or "touching the hot iron caused me to feel pain" is just that the former kind of event is always followed by the latter kind. Unfortunately, this view as it stands is clearly hopeless. (Imagine that when I flip a switch, two lights – A and B – go on, one just after the other. The illumination of A is constantly conjoined with the illumination of B, but of course the former is not a *cause* of the latter; rather, they are both common effects of my flipping the switch.) But most of the major theories of causation that were developed in the latter part of the twentieth century retain the guiding thought that causation reduces to regularity – they just make the story much more complicated in order to avoid this kind of counter-example. Statistical relevance theories, John Mackie's INUS condition account, and David Lewis's counterfactual theory all belong in this category.

Lewis, as perhaps the most significant single contributor to analytic philosophy over the past forty years or so, constitutes one piece of evidence for the claim I made earlier about Hume's influence on philosophy. Lewis himself conceives of a good deal of his own philosophy as contributing to Hume's agenda, and names one of his most significant philosophical theses – Humean supervenience – after the man he calls the "greater denier of necessary connections". Humean supervenience is, roughly, the thesis that the world is, at bottom, a mosaic of unconnected "matters of particular fact", and that the connections we talk about – such as causal relations – depend on this pattern (which includes patterns of regularity or "constant conjunctions"). Hence the "Humean" in "Humean supervenience": for Lewis, as for Hume (at least on some interpretations of Hume), there are no necessary connections in nature. Indeed, one might see the cornerstone of Lewis's whole philosophical system – "modal realism" – as an aspect of this denial of necessary connections in nature. Lewis holds that modal facts – such as facts about necessity and possibility, as well as ⧉⧉⧉

Causation is a product of the imagination

counterfactuals ("if *A* had been the case, then *B* would have been the case") – are really facts about what is true across "possible worlds". For example, to say that something is necessary is to say that it is true in all possible worlds. So this conception of modality itself enshrines a commitment to the thesis of "no necessary connections in nature" – since to say that, for example, something happens *of necessity* is not to say something about the intrinsic nature of the actual world (that is, the world we inhabit) but rather it is to say something about what happens across all possible worlds. Thus we can happily make claims about necessity without thinking that necessity is a feature of any *particular* possible world, including our own.

The continental tradition, of course, took a rather different tack – one that can be traced directly back to Kant and, through him, to Hume. Kant charmingly described causation on Hume's view a "bastard of the imagination, impregnated by experience". For Hume, causation is a product of the imagination, in the sense that the imagination is the mental faculty that, via the custom or habit that prompts our inference from causes to effect, produces the impression, and hence the idea, of necessary connection; and the imagination is "impregnated by experience" in the sense that is past experience of constant conjunction that sets up this habit. As you might have guessed from Kant's description of Hume's view, he wasn't

a big fan. For Kant, Hume gets the order of explanation the wrong way round. Hume, being an empiricist, thought that all of our ideas (or concepts), including the idea of causation, come from experience (or "impressions") – so it is our experience that explains how we come to have the concepts (such as causation) that we do. (In the case of causation, though, the impression of necessary connection is an "impression of reflection" rather than a sensory impression: its source lies in the operation of our minds and not our senses.) Kant thought this was all back-to-front: we need to have the concept of causation, among others, in order to be capable of having any experience at all. So, according to Kant, that concept cannot itself be the product of experience, but must have its source in the "pure understanding".

One way to see the broader dispute between Hume and Kant – and the way Kant saw it – is to think about the status of metaphysics as a branch of philosophical enquiry. Hume's view was that we cannot go beyond experience when it comes to investigating the nature of reality. Take, for example, the principle that every event has a cause. On Hume's view (arguably at any rate; nearly every claim one makes about Hume's views has been disputed by at least one interpreter), we have good evidence that this principle is true, since all the events we have ever observed have indeed had causes. But our evidence is strictly empirical, and so the principle is capable of empirical refutation. And what goes for this principle goes across the board: *a priori* metaphysics – the study of reality via principles that are established solely on the basis of *a priori* reasoning or pure thought – is nonsense. Or, as Hume put it: "Consign it then to the flames: For it can contain nothing but sophistry and illusion". A major aim of Kant's *Critique of Pure Reason* was to re-establish metaphysics as "the Queen of all the sciences": since it turns out that concepts such as causation are the product of the pure understanding, metaphysical principles (for example, the principle that every event has a cause) can after all be established *a priori*. Thus metaphysics can be rescued from Hume's bonfire.

The downside, however, is that these principles that we can know *a priori* – and indeed any claim we can meaningfully make about the world at all – will apply only to (as Kant sometimes puts it) "objects of experience" (or "phenomena") and not to "things in themselves" (noumena). So Kant is what is sometimes known as "transcendental idealist". We can have no knowledge of – and

indeed (at least on some interpretations of Kant) cannot even formulate meaningful claims about – things in themselves, because our concepts can only apply to objects of experience, and not to whatever it is that lies behind those experiences. For example, we can't even say that our experiences of the world are *caused* by things in themselves. Causation is one of the *a priori* concepts or "categories" that determine how

There are no necessary connections in nature

we experience and conceptualise the world; we therefore cannot meaningfully apply it to unconceptualised, noumenal reality.

Kant's transcendental idealism was the starting-point for the "German idealism" of philosophers such as Fichte and Hegel. Kant is thus sometimes thought of the father (or perhaps the grandfather) of continental philosophy. So, given that Kant's idealism was itself a direct response to Hume's empiricism, we can perhaps think of Hume as its grandfather (or maybe its great-grandfather), albeit one who would not have entirely approved of his distant descendants.

The same might be said, however, of some of Hume's distant descendants on the analytic side. Interestingly, despite its deep roots in Hume's empiricism, quite a lot of contemporary analytic metaphysics would appear to assume that we can do something that neither Hume nor Kant thought was possible: we can investigate the nature of the world in itself just by thinking about it from the philosopher's armchair. Hume and Kant would have been united in their suspicion of such "speculative metaphysics".

Popular religions are practical; they are used as guides to living. But philosophical religion has *no* implications for how we should live. Hume thought that philosophical theism and popular monotheism cannot be coherently united. Yet incoherent unification is precisely what has happened in our own culture.

Design flaws

HUME'S CONSIDERATION OF INTELLIGENT DESIGN STILL MATTERS, ARGUES MARTIN BELL

As this year is the 300th anniversary of David Hume's birth, it is a good time to ask how his philosophy still matters. Something that mattered a lot to Hume was religion, and I think that what he said about it remains important today. Hume's ideas do relate to traditional areas of philosophy like metaphysics, and he does discuss things like the traditional proofs of the existence of God. But he puts this in the context of his overall project: to develop a "science of man" or "theory of human nature". The science of man is, he says, fundamental to understanding all forms of human thought and action, including philosophy in our modern sense. For example, metaphysical

Martin Bell is emeritus professor of history of philosophy at Manchester Metropolitan University and chair of the British Society for the History of Philosophy

proofs or refutations of the existence of God are intended to satisfy reason. But what is human reason, and what are its powers and limits? That is a prior question, and it is about the nature of human reason, a part of human nature.

Hume bases his theory of human nature on observation and experience. He claims it is an empirical theory. Evidence for it is the sorts of experiences anyone might have in perceiving, remembering, imagining, feeling, experiencing emotions, thinking and so on. Evidence also comes from historical records of human life and the experience of other people. But Hume disregards histories inspired by religious ideas, such as stories of the creation of human beings by divine power. He thinks of humans as being simply natural creatures alongside other forms of life on earth, not as specially created "in the image of God". Whereas many of his predecessors thought human reason is unique because it is a reflection of divine reason, Hume emphasised the similarities between human reason and the reason of animals. This secular approach means not assuming religious teachings and traditions as premises. For instance, we cannot take it for granted that human reason is a guide to truth on the basis that it is God-given, a kind of "divine light". Instead we have to examine how reason works in practice to discover its strengths and weaknesses. Part of Hume's fame or notoriety rests here, because he showed that some of the most basic beliefs we have about our experience – such as the belief that the everyday objects we perceive in our environment exist independently of our perceiving them – cannot be proved true simply by reason. In fact Hume argued that there are a number of such basic everyday beliefs – beliefs in terms of which we live, yet beliefs which we cannot prove. They are, so to speak, part of human nature.

Living by beliefs that you can't prove might sound a bit like religious belief. So, does Hume accept that religious belief is part of human nature? His answer is: not at the most fundamental level of being human. The main reason is that religious beliefs are very varied. Religions are human inventions, and take different forms in different places and times, like many other aspects of human life and culture. In such cases there will probably be found some underlying universal and, as he puts it, "original" features of human nature, such as instincts and biological needs, but these lead to "secondary" cultural practices. Secondary cultural practices come from the interplay between "original" features of human nature and what he calls "circumstances". Because religious beliefs depend in part on "circumstances", Hume writes about them in

a quasi historical way in *The Natural History of Religion*. This book gives a sort of conjectural or speculative account of how religions might have started and developed in human history. What matters for us here are not the details, which contemporary anthropologists and sociologists of religion find often crude, simplistic or unconvincing, but the model Hume gave of how to think of religions in a naturalistic, secular way, and the philosophical significance this has.

Religions are human inventions, like other aspects of culture

The book begins with a distinction between two questions. The first asks what rational basis there is for religious beliefs. The second asks what the origin of religion in human nature is. The reply to the first is that religious belief is based on reason so far as it comes from pure curiosity about the cause of the regularity and order of the world. We notice that Hume allows only one kind of rational argument for religious belief to count, what looks like an inference from the regularity and order of the world considered as an effect to (presumably) a divine cause of that effect. He does not make room for other rational arguments like ontological or first cause arguments. It's clear from other writings that Hume does not think these other arguments are valid, so they do not provide a rational basis. As to the argument from the regularity and order of the world, Hume's point is that only a few people in the history of the world can have been in a position to appreciate the regularity and order of the world, and ⇛

to have the leisure to contemplate it with a pure curiosity. Religious belief of that kind, based solely on such rational considerations, must be relatively recent in human

history. Hume calls it "pure theism", and says that early humans and contemporary "primitive" peoples cannot be thought to have shared it. On the contrary, the first and earliest form of religion, he maintains, must have been polytheistic. Why? Because the origin of religion in human nature depends not on reason but on natural human emotions of hope and fear caused by the fluctuations of fortune. That is combined with ignorance of the causes of these fluctuations. In the absence of rational understanding of the order of nature, the human imagination tries to give itself objects of hope and fear by inventing ideas of invisible intelligent agents who are the causes of the kinds of events that arouse the emotions. This is the birth of what Hume calls "polytheism or idolatry".

Polytheistic religions are the product of hopes and fears in conditions of ignorance aided by the imagination. That is very different from Hume's "pure theism", produced by detached contemplation and curiosity in conditions of scientific understanding. Hume calls all religions that arise from human nature, as polytheism does, "popular" religions. Yet, he says, popular religions are not all polytheist. Monotheism, a belief in a unique deity, can arise from polytheism. Fear usually overpowers hope in the formation of religious beliefs. People want to placate and flatter the deities. Giving one deity precedence over the others placates and flatters that deity. The idea

of a supreme deity can gradually lead to the idea of a single, unique deity. Monotheism is also a form of popular religion.

Readers today are not likely to buy the details of Hume's natural history of religion. But it was at the time revolutionary, and it leads to conclusions that certainly are important today. At the time, it was quite common to hold that polytheism and what was usually called "superstition" were corruptions of an original pure religion revealed by God himself. Hume's natural history turns the story round. Polytheism and superstition is the original form of religion. Monotheism emerges at a later stage. And although he could not risk being too explicit, Hume was saying that *popular* monotheisms such as Judaism, Islam and Christianity are descendants of polytheism and superstition. Did Hume think that these popular religions are corruptions and, if so, of what? I think part of the answer is that Hume thought popular monotheisms were harder for our imaginations to grasp than were ancient polytheisms, and for that reason involve a kind of pretence. He thought that believers in these religions often do not really believe what they say. Another part of the answer is that he also thought that popular monotheisms were both corrupted by and corrupted philosophical reasoning of the kind on which it seems "pure theism" would be based.

This takes us to the heart of what still matters today in Hume's philosophy of religion. The point is this. Popular religions, both polytheist and monotheist, arise from emotions. These arise from facing the ups and downs of life. Popular religions are practical; they are used as guides to living. But "pure theism", which could be called philosophical religion, has *no* implications for how we should live. That is a major proposition, and we have yet to see why Hume put it forward. But assuming it is correct we can understand why Hume thought that philosophical theism and popular monotheism cannot be coherently united. Yet incoherent unification is precisely what has happened in our own culture. Philosophical reasoning is appealed to in order to justify not "pure theism" but the doctrines of monotheistic religions that promise to tell us how to live. In Hume's eyes, this combination of philosophy and theology is absurd, and corrupts both understanding and morality.

What we need to consider, then, is Hume's major claim: that there can be no philosophical basis for religious doctrines that claim to teach us how to live. Let us first consider just how crucial this claim is. If Hume is right, philosophical – and for Hume this would include scientific in our modern sense – arguments about what caused the order and regularity of the world cannot yield conclusions that have any practical implications for how we ought to live. Suppose you think that the order and regularity of the world is sufficient evidence to conclude that it was "designed" by some kind of "intelligence". For Hume this could not give you any reason whatever to live a virtuous life or a vicious

life. It could not give you any reason whatever to take part in or to avoid religious ceremonies and practices. Someone convinced that the cause of the order and regularity of the world is some kind of intelligence has no more reason than has someone who denies it to live a morally good life.

To put it crudely, Hume thinks it does not really *matter* whether you do or do not claim that the universe was created by a divine intelligence. And I think that it is because of this claim that

It does not really *matter* whether you claim the universe was created

Hume's philosophy of religion is still important to us.

Some of Hume's readers are concerned by the fact that in *The Natural History of Religion* Hume seems confident that the argument from the order and regularity of the world to a divine designer is forceful, while in other writings he expressed severe doubts about the argument. But that overlooks the main point – Hume thinks that what matters is that the argument cannot give us any conclusions about how to live. So let us look briefly at what he says about this famous argument, the design argument.

The first thing is that it is an argument from an effect (the order and regularity of the world) to a cause. Hume's analysis of the idea of causation and of the nature of arguments from causes and effects appears at the heart of his first book, *A Treatise of Human Nature*. He shows that we learn what things are causes of what effects only from observation and experience. Knowing that the temperature of the water in the kettle ⊳⊳⊳

will rise when we put it over the fire is not like knowing that 6 is the sum of 4 and 2. Next, the kind of observation and experience we need to work out what causes what effects is repetition of cases. When things happen in a regular order we come to expect that order to be repeated next time. We are prone to think that one thing is the cause of another only after we have experience of how things of that kind behave.

In the case of the order and regularity of the world, what experience do we have by which to conclude that the cause is a divine intelligence? None, for we have no experience of other cases. But perhaps that conclusion is too quick. Could we not argue that the order and regularity of the world is *like* the order and regularity of a machine, such as a clock? We do have experience of what causes the order and regularity of the movements of the clock – human design. So by analogy we could say that the cause in the case of the world is *like* a human designer. In his *Dialogues Concerning Natural Religion* Hume enjoys subjecting this analogy to various challenges, some quite credible others rather far fetched. For example, many complex engineering projects require the collaboration of numerous designers. Perhaps the universe was built by a committee of deities?

However, the central point that Hume emphasises about causal arguments like these is as follows. If we know the features of the effect which we want to be explained, then we need to be able to infer a cause capable of producing those features. But we cannot then say that the cause has *other* capacities beyond those required to produce the effect. Let us apply this to the case of divine intelligence and the order and regularity of the world. We might concede that the divine intelligence exists, and has the power to produce the world as it is. But the world as it is provides no evidence that the divine intelligence has *other* features, such as a determination to reward virtuous people with eternal happiness in an afterlife. Hume is prepared to concede that there might be a cause of the order and regularity of the world that is in some vague and indefinable way like human intelligence. But he strongly denies that the way the world is provides *any* evidence from which to infer that the divine designer cares one way or the other about how human beings live their lives.

That is why Hume teaches us not to confuse popular religions, which offer us ways of living, with philosophical speculations about the cause of the order and regularity of the world, which can never lead to any conclusions about how we ought to live. The strengths and weaknesses of the argument for intelligent design are matters for philosophy and science. But so far as deciding how to live and dealing with the ups and downs of existence are concerned, the argument has nothing to contribute. In view of the fact that for most people the whole point of religious belief is to support, console and inspire us in our lives, one can say that Hume's importance for us lies in what he has shown: philosophical reasoning cannot provide any support for practical religion.

A radical implication of Hume's theory of motivation is that it makes no sense, strictly speaking, to call actions rational or irrational. So, he claims, it is not contrary to reason for me to prefer the destruction of the world to getting a scratch on my finger.

Ruling passions

ELIZABETH S RADCLIFFE EXPLAINS HOW HUME PUT FEELINGS CENTRE STAGE

We've probably all had the experience of being on the verge of acting from anger or jealousy, when someone advises us to act reasonably. A typical picture of motivation for action is one in which emotions or desires drive us one way and our reason drives us in another. I have a desire for a tasty but unhealthy dessert, and the voice of reason tells me that I ought not to eat it. I don't feel like helping at the food bank on Saturday, but conscience tells me that I ought to fulfil my obligation. On this picture, the morally upstanding or prudent person follows the lead of reason, while the morally deficient character caves into desire or emotion.

David Hume, in *A Treatise of Human Nature*, rejects this traditional characterisation of action and its evaluation, offering a remarkable theory in response. He defends the views that the ends or goals of our actions in all cases are given by our "passions", not by reason, and that the practical role of reason is to figure out how to fulfil these goals. He makes the astounding declaration that "Reason is, and ought only to be the slave of the passions, and can never pretend to any other office than to serve and obey them." Subsequently, Hume also rejects the analysis of morality in terms of rationality, and argues that our distinctions between virtue and vice are based on shared sentiments or feelings of approval or disapproval we experience towards persons' characters.

Elizabeth S Radcliffe is professor of philosophy at the College of William and Mary, president of the Hume Society, and author of *Hume, Passion, and Action* (Oxford University Press, forthcoming)

Although Hume wrote in the eighteenth century, his philosophy has significant implications for questions posed in contemporary motivational psychology and moral philosophy. In fact, Hume's work stimulated one of the classical and still ongoing debates in practical reasoning, concerning whether our goals are created by reason and subject to its evaluation, or whether our goals come from feelings or passions. Moreover, his sentimentalist moral

"Reason is, and ought only to be the slave of the passions"

theory is the inspiration for contemporary discussions in ethics, such as those presented in Michael Slote's *Moral Sentimentalism*, and Jesse Prinz's *The Emotional Construction of Morals*. How did Hume reach his significant conclusions, and what impact did they have on the course of philosophy at the time in which he defended them?

One of the major intellectual and practical advances of the seventeenth century was the development of a distinct scientific method. David Hume's announced project was to implement this newly developed scientific method in an empirical study of human nature. Hume's study included the explanation of human actions and the motives for them, and an investigation into why we make the moral distinctions among actions and motives in the way that we do. In applying the scientific approach to these topics, Hume's intent was to put explanations of action and morality on the same basis as other natural phenomena, looking for explanations of them

in terms of a few fundamental natural principles, rather than by appealing to supernatural or religious events. Accordingly, he characterised reason not as some mysterious power of grasping truth or of intuiting connections between ideas or thoughts, as some philosophers did, but as the ability either to offer demonstrations or proofs or to make causal inferences.

So, first, he shows that reason engaged in demonstration can never be a motive to action. Demonstration is deductive reasoning using necessary truths. Demonstrations are the proofs we use in mathematics and geometry. Mathematics can be applied to the world in the way that engineers use it to solve problems in their work, but knowing the truths of mathematics only, without the addition of a goal or purpose, will not produce a motive to any particular action. Second, Hume asks whether causal reasoning by itself can motivate action. Causal reasoning, which requires the gathering and assembling of observations, allows us to form beliefs about the world. Do these factual beliefs supply us with motivation to act in particular ways? Say I'm sleepy and I believe coffee can stimulate me. It seems this belief can motivate me to drink a cup of coffee. If so, factual beliefs based on causal reasoning can on their own produce motives. However, Hume notices that such beliefs would have no practical effect on us if we didn't also have some sort of attraction to the goal achieved by the motivated action – in this instance, staying awake when I'm feeling sleepy. Reason informs me that consuming the caffeine in coffee keeps me awake, but reason didn't tell me what desires to have. It simply gives me a piece of causal information. Factual beliefs have no influence on our behaviour if they are about things in the world of no concern to us.

The concern or motivation necessary to action originates, Hume argues, with passions, which are either feelings prompted by sources of pleasure and pain or instincts that produce pleasure or pain. Among the former are desire, fear, and anger. Among the latter are benevolence, thirst and love of life, but there are many other passions as well. Since reason cannot prompt action, it cannot oppose passion over what we are to do. The only way something can be opposed to passion is by initiating a motivation in a contrary direction. This is why the popular model mentioned at the beginning and accepted among some seventeenth-century rationalists is overturned by Hume's arguments.

If the impetus to action always originates with a passion, then why does it look as though beliefs, which come from reason, can sometimes make our passions come and go? For instance, a mother fears that her child has been killed by kidnappers. Her fears are turned to joy when the police phone her with the information that he has been found uninjured at a nearby park. Hume himself emphasises that beliefs are practical and have an impact on our emotions. Nonetheless, in any case, we will always find some initial passions, originated without reason, with which beliefs cooperate. In the case of a mother's fear turned to joy, her beliefs affect her emotions only because she has an underlying affection for her child, itself not originated by reason.

A radical implication of Hume's theory of motivation is that it makes no sense, strictly speaking, to call actions rational or irrational. Since they are caused by passions, which cannot be so evaluated, there is no basis on which to apply these terms to actions. So, he claims, it is not contrary to reason for me to prefer the destruction of the world to getting a scratch on my finger; it is not irrational for me to undermine my long-term good for a trivial short-term pleasure. His view sounds astoundingly implausible at first. But consider: he is not saying that actions are subject to no evaluations whatsoever. Actions *are* the objects of moral judgment. It is surely vicious of me to allow others to be destroyed in order to save myself a small inconvenience. It is definitely imprudent of me to avoid my dental appointment for a root canal today, when such behaviour will result in larger health problems for me later. Hume argues that this simply means that our moral evaluations are done on some basis besides reason.

While Hume was not the first philosopher to suggest that ends of actions cannot come from reason (Aristotle, for instance, attributed them to a wish), his scientific precision and rigour have made his arguments the touchstone for subsequent debates on this topic. Contemporary philosophers working in action theory identify themselves as Humean or anti-Humean, depending on whether they subscribe to the "belief–desire" model of motivation descended from Hume. The belief–desire model says that both mental states are required for action: a desire to set an aim and a belief about how to achieve that aim. Anti-Humeans, often descended from Immanuel Kant, still argue that reason can and ought to have authority over our desires. Some maintain, despite Hume's arguments, that we can use reason to decide what ends to adopt, by examining our desires and determining which are consistent with the demands of rationality. Contemporary Humeans, in response, spend ⋙

a great deal of effort attempting to develop a theory true to Hume's tenets, but one that allows (contrary to Hume) that our actions *can* be reasonable or unreasonable. On one approach, desires that the agent values more than other desires determine better reasons for action.

Hume's proposals in ethics were also innovative. One of his opponents, Samuel Clarke, had claimed in his famous Boyle Lectures of 1705

We sympathise to a greater degree with those who resemble us

that the universe has a rational structure to which only certain events and actions are fitting. Actions done contrary to reason are morally wrong, and it is self-evident when they are wrong. For instance, it requires no experience, Clarke argues, to know that it is fitter to promote the welfare of other people than to destroy them. Hume thinks that Clarke misrepresents reason as a mystical power of discernment. On the scientific notion of reason, reason can't move us on its own. Since the point of making moral judgements is to affect or motivate behaviour, the conclusion we must accept as naturalists is that moral judgements are not based on reason by itself. If it is wrong to destroy other people without provocation (and Hume agrees that it is), it is not because doing so runs up against a rational order.

Hume proposed that our moral distinctions must come from the non-rational, sensitive part of our nature. This conclusion leads Hume at one point to say that our moral distinctions come from a moral "sense", as though we perceive

moral goodness or badness by a special sense in the way that we perceive colours and tastes by the physical senses. To what extent Hume thinks that we actually have a moral sense is debatable. Hume clearly thinks our moral distinctions depend upon our sensitive reactions, though: when we feel approval (a pleasure or satisfaction) towards a person, we judge her as virtuous, and when we feel disapproval (a pain or dissatisfaction), we judge him as vicious.

In the attempt to explain our mental life in terms of a few naturalistic principles, Hume argues that the fundamental principle of sympathy underlies our moral judgements. It is not an exaggeration to say that, of all philosophers, Hume most highlighted the role of sympathy in ordinary life. The economist, moral philosopher, and friend to Hume Adam Smith probably places second in understanding the importance of sympathy to human interactions. Sympathy is the capacity to experience feelings similar to others' feelings by thinking about what they are experiencing. We infer the feelings of others from their behaviour; this idea of their feelings takes on a greater forcefulness as we imagine ourselves affected by the circumstances of others' situations. I drive by the scene of a terrible car accident, and I cringe at the thought of the bodies in the twisted wreckage; the thought of their suffering causes me psychological pain. When I think about a heinous murderer, the explanation of my disapproval, which is a form of discomfort, is that I sympathise with the victims of the murderer's actions, and I know that the victims suffered greatly.

We don't, however, sympathise to the same extent with all human beings. One of Hume's observations about human nature is that we sympathise to a greater degree with those who are close to us, resemble us, or are related to us. Hume says that I won't feel the same lively pleasure from the virtues of a person who lived in Greece 2,000 years ago as I feel from the virtues of a familiar acquaintance. We are more affected by the feelings of those with whom we find something in common than by the feelings of those with whom we share little, because the resemblances between us makes it easier to imagine the others' feelings. But if such sympathetic feelings are the foundation of our moral judgements, does it follow that our moral judgements are subjective?

Hume answers that in order to communicate about morality and avoid practical problems arising from conflicting moral judgements, we consider our sympathetic feelings indicative of moral distinctions *only* when we take up a generally shared perspective on an action or character. In so doing, we consider the effects of an action or character in isolation from our personal connections to the actor. More specifically, the common point of view from which we make moral distinctions is the viewpoint of one who sympathises with the circle of people most directly affected by the agent's actions. The spectator's feelings must mirror the feelings of those who are the direct recipients of the agent's actions and their consequences. For instance, when I make a moral judgement about a dictator in a distant country, I think about the effects on the citizens there and identify with their feelings; I try to do it in the same way I think about and respond to the effects of my local government on citizens here. In each case, I identify only with the feelings of people directly affected by the government actions.

Hume's moral theory is not just a descriptive account about how we make moral judgements; it also has normative implications. His is a spectator theory of the virtues. A character trait is virtuous if an observer approves, through sympathy, of the effects of that trait on others from the common perspective; a character trait is a vice if such an observer disapproves. Hume notes that we will find a natural division among the approved features, the virtues. One class consists of those that make a person able to promote his or her own interests; the other consists of those that make a person fit for society. In *An Enquiry Concerning the Principles of Morals* Hume details these virtues and vices. Among the qualities "immediately agreeable" to the self are cheerfulness, tranquillity and serenity. Qualities useful to society include generosity, gratitude, kindness and courage; and qualities immediately agreeable to others are politeness, wit, ingenuity, modesty, decency and cleanliness.

In addition to combating the moral rationalism popular in the seventeenth century, Hume's moral theory had the profound effect of undermining the "selfish" school of thought propagated at the time by Hobbes and Mandeville, who alleged that all human behaviour was motivated entirely by self-interest. While sentimentalism was becoming more popular in the eighteenth century owing to writers like Shaftesbury and Hutcheson, Hume became the most dynamic representative of the theory. Twenty-first-century moral controversies over the importance of emotions and sympathy versus rationality and duty refer constantly to Hume's opinions. Popular discussions of moral sensibility in venues like James Q Wilson's *The Moral Sense* owe a huge debt to the philosopher whose systematic study of human nature revealed that the moral life is a life with feelings at the centre stage.

We might be inclined to think of the mind as a kind of theatre in which our thoughts and feelings – or "perceptions" – make their appearance; but if so we are misled, for the mind is *constituted* by its perceptions.

Sure of your self?

TONY PITSON ON HUME'S PROVOCATIVE ACCOUNT OF WHAT WE REALLY ARE

Hume's account of the self is to be found mainly in one short and provocative section of his *Treatise of Human Nature* – a landmark work in the history of philosophy, published when Hume was still a young man. What Hume says here (in "Of Personal Identity") has provoked a philosophical debate that continues to this day. What, then, is so novel and striking about Hume's account that would explain its fascination for generations of philosophers?

One of the problems of personal identity has to do with what it is for you to remain the same person over time. In recalling your childhood experiences, or looking forward to your next holiday, it appears that in each case you are thinking about one and the same person – namely, *you*. But what makes this true? The same sort of question might be raised about an object such as the house in which you're now living. Perhaps it has undergone various changes from the time when you first moved in – and you may have plans to alter it further. But you probably think that it is the same house throughout. So how is this so? It helps in this case that at least we're pretty clear about what it is for something to be a house (namely, a building with a certain function), and therefore to be the *same* house through time. But what is it for you to be a person (or self)? This is the question with which Hume begins. He is keen to dismiss the prevailing philosophical answer to this question – one that perhaps also reflects common ways of thinking. The view to which Hume is referring is that underlying our various thoughts and feelings is a core self: the *soul*, as it is

Tony Pitson is honorary research fellow in the department of philosophy, University of Stirling, and author of *Hume's Philosophy of the Self* (Routledge, 2002)

sometimes referred to. This notion also appears to provide an answer to our question about personal identity. For the soul is supposed to connect our mental states so that they belong to one and the same person. As the subject of our mental states the soul is apparently to be distinguished from the body though, like the body itself, it is a kind of thing, albeit a non-material one. This way of thinking about the self is associated with belief in life after death; for it is the soul that is supposed to be capable of surviving the death of the body.

How, then, does Hume respond to this view of the self? An important philosophical principle for Hume is that where claims of existence are involved it is necessary to consult experience. Any intelligible idea of ourselves must derive from what Hume calls an "impression" – a kind of conscious representation. So far as the self is concerned it seems that the only source of evidence available is provided by introspection. According to Hume, however, when we introspect consciousness fails to reveal any such thing as the soul is supposed to be. What, then, *is* it of which we are aware when we consult experience by looking inwards at ourselves? The answer, according to Hume, is that we only ever encounter "perceptions" – mental states that include not only ordinary perceptual experiences but also the thoughts, feelings and so on that make up the contents of our minds. It is these, and these alone, that are the objects of self-awareness. Hume concludes memorably that each of us is "nothing but a bundle or collection of different perceptions". We might be inclined to think of the mind as a kind of theatre in which our thoughts and feelings – or "perceptions" – make their appearance; but if so we are misled,

for the mind is *constituted* by its perceptions. This is the famous "bundle" theory of the mind or self that Hume offers as his alternative to the doctrine of the soul.

A number of questions arise here. Hume himself seems to concede that the doctrine he rejects is not entirely removed from our ordinary ways of thinking. For we find it quite natural to suppose that our mental states are connected by

The soul is supposed to be capable of surviving death

something "unknown and mysterious" even if we do not use the word "soul" to refer to it. How is this to be accounted for if, as Hume claims, it involves a mistaken view of the self? Hume in fact provides an ingenious and rather complicated psychological explanation of our tendency to run into this view. The gist of what he says is that we take ourselves to remain the same over time in spite of variations and interruptions in our mental states, and we feign the existence of something connecting these states (in philosophical terms, the soul) so as to disguise their variations and interruptions. But what of Hume's alternative to the doctrine of the soul?

A natural question to raise about his bundle theory is how it is possible for mental states to exist without belonging to something apart from the states themselves. Surely, a thought, for example, cannot just exist in its own right independently of that which thinks it? Hume appears to agree that experience shows our "perceptions" in fact to be incapable of an independent existence. But he would deny that the doctrine of the soul provides a way of explaining this fact about ⟩⟩⟩

Surely, a thought cannot just exist in its own right

our mental states. The doctrine represents the mind or self as an immaterial thing or substance. But, Hume argues, we are unable to form any meaningful idea of the self so considered. For this would depend on our having some corresponding impression (or conscious representation), and it seems evident that no such impression is available to us. What, then, does Hume have to offer in place of the soul doctrine as an account of the ownership of mental states?

Hume's own view is that our mental states are causally dependent on the body (rather than a separate mind or soul). This requires him to reject a number of principles associated with the doctrine of the soul. One of these is that the nature of our thoughts or feelings requires us to ascribe them to something immaterial rather than to the body as a physical object. The result is a dualist account of mind and body as proposed by Descartes. While Hume accepts that some of our "perceptions", at least, may not have any

physical location this does not, he argues, prevent them from being effects of bodily occurrences. The crucial point is that the nature of their relation to the body is a factual issue – and issues of this kind can be settled only by reference to experience, not by appeal to arguments about what it is possible for us to conceive. This bears on Hume's view of the nature of *causation*.

Some proponents of the doctrine of the soul appeal to the principle that a causal relation between two things is possible only if there is a resemblance between our *ideas* of these things. And it is suggested that a supposed causal relation between the body (physical) and thought (mental) violates this principle. But, Hume insists, "anything may be the cause or effect of anything": we simply cannot say in advance of experience what objects or events may be related as cause and effect, however different our ideas of them may be from each other. If two kinds of thing are regularly conjoined we may

presume that they are causally related no matter what these things are. And, Hume suggests, we find that our mental states *are* conjoined in this way with bodily events such as "motions" in the brain. If it is objected that there appears to be no *connection* between thoughts and such motions, the same might be said, according to Hume, of relations of cause and effect in general. We may think that there is always some necessary connection between events so related, but Hume claims that no such connection is ever revealed in experience.

Hume is well aware that what he has to say here about the relation of mental states to the body has important and controversial ramifications. As I have indicated, the doctrine of the soul tends to be associated with belief in life after death, to the extent that the self is represented as something immaterial which is capable of existing independently of the body. Hume responds to this aspect of the doctrine in an essay, "Of the Immortality of the Soul", suppressed for prudential reasons during his lifetime. He notes here that several different kinds of argument have been put forward in support of the belief in an immortal soul. One of these is precisely the kind of metaphysical argument alluded to above, which is supposed to establish that thought cannot belong to anything material but must be ascribed to an independently existing immaterial or spiritual substance. Hume again insists that abstract reasoning cannot determine whether or not matter may be the cause of thought; and he adds that "arguments from the analogy of nature" favour not only the dependence of thought on the body but also our mortality. When we fall asleep our minds undergo a kind of "temporary extinction"; and, more generally, our bodily health and strength significantly affect mental functioning. But it seems reasonable to infer that when there is an especially dramatic alteration in the state of our body – in fact, its dissolution – so also there will be a dramatic effect on the mind or self, namely, its ceasing to exist.

The case of non-human animals is relevant in this context. To the extent that they, like us, have thoughts and feelings we might wonder why the doctrine of the soul would not also apply

Did Hume accept his own mortality?

to them. Should they not be granted immaterial and immortal souls? If we resist this conclusion in spite of the many respects in which they resemble us mentally, then their presumed mortality appears to lead by an argument from analogy to the conclusion that we also are mortal beings.

It is natural to wonder how far this aspect of what Hume says about the self is reflected in his own life. Did he accept his own mortality? And, if so, did he not then fear death? We have evidence on these matters both from Johnson's biographer, James Boswell, and also Hume's friend and fellow philosopher Adam Smith. Boswell relates that he visited Hume shortly before his death and raised the question of whether he still rejected the idea of an afterlife. Hume made it clear that he continued to think that it was quite unreasonable to believe that we should exist forever. Nor did the thought of his death cause him any uneasiness. Here Hume cited the reference by the poet Lucretius to what Epicurus said about the fear of death. According to Epicurus there is a ⋙

What does Hume have to offer in place of the soul?

symmetrical relation between our non-existence before we were born and our non-existence after death. We don't consider our not having existed for an eternity before birth as a terrible thing. So why should our not existing for an eternity after death be considered an evil?

This is reflected in Hume's own attitude towards death. Hume told Boswell that he had no wish to live forever and that he did not find the idea of an afterlife a pleasing one. Boswell remarks that Hume remained in good humour throughout their conversation and his equanimity in the face of death was confirmed by Smith, who records in a letter that Hume endured his last illness in cheerful conversation and games of cards with his friends. (Hume also continued to make corrections for new editions of his philo-sophical writings until shortly before his death.)

To return briefly to Hume's "bundle" theory, it amounts to a *reductionist* view of the self. In other words, the existence of the self consists in the existence of certain other things – our mental states or "perceptions". The contrast here is with the doctrine of the soul, according to which the mind as an immaterial substance is irreducibly different from anything else that exists. A non-reductionist view of this kind might well object to the alternative provided by Hume, that far from providing an account of the self, it amounts in effect to denying that it exists. Reference to a "bundle" (Hume also uses the word "heap") of "perceptions" scarcely seems to capture anything we might recognise as constituting the existence of a person or self.

Fortunately Hume offers an analogy that perhaps helps to make his reductionist view more convincing. Consider the example of a nation. It will consist in a number of individual members or citizens united together by such things as the laws and constitutions under which they are governed. Of course the members of the nation will change, and its laws and constitution may also change over time. Yet we continue to regard it as the same nation even though, arguably, there is nothing more to its being the nation it is than the citizens who compose it and the institutions that govern their relations with each other.

Hume suggests that we should think of ourselves in just the same sort of way. Our mental states obviously change considerably from one time to another; and even relatively stable features of our mental lives, such as our char-acters or dispositions, may undergo change. Yet we continue to think of ourselves as remaining the same in spite of such changes. The explana-tion, according to Hume, is that there are certain important relations among our mental states just as there are among the citizens of a nation. In the case of the mind or self, our ability to remember experiences results in *resemblances* among our mental states (my thought of a past experience resembles that experience to the extent that it really is a memory of it); and, more significantly, there are also relations of *causation* among our states of mind (for example, I see that you are in distress, I feel pity for you, and the strength of my sympathy moves me to go to your aid). When the self or mind is considered from this point of view it amounts, in Hume's phrase, to a "system of different perceptions": one that exhibits psychological continuities that arguably account for the identity we ascribe to ourselves as persons.

There is undoubtedly much in the above account of the self that might be considered puzzling and strange, although aspects of it may be found in contemporary treatments of personal identity, and it is sometimes claimed that Hume's theory bears comparison with the Buddhist view of the self. It is noteworthy that Hume himself appears to express dissatisfaction with what he says about personal identity, although the nature of his second thoughts is a matter of controversy. But even from this relatively brief survey of what Hume has to say about the self, it is perhaps evident why this aspect of his philosophy, along with so much else of what it contains, remains the subject of vigorous philosophical debate.

forum/self

95

Hume on personal identity

"For my part, when I enter most intimately into what I call *myself*, I always stumble on some particular perception or other, of heat or cold, light or shade, love or hatred, pain or pleasure. I never can catch *myself* at any time without a perception, and never can observe any thing but the perception. When my perceptions are remov'd for any time, as by sound sleep; so long am I insensible of *myself*, and may truly be said not to exist. And were all my perceptions remov'd by death, and cou'd I neither think, nor feel, nor see, nor love, nor hate after the dissolution of my body, I shou'd be entirely annihilated, nor do I conceive what is farther requisite to make me a perfect non-entity. If any one upon serious and unprejudic'd reflexion, thinks he has a different notion of *himself*, I must confess I can reason no longer with him. All I can allow him is, that he may be in the right as well as I, and that we are essentially different in this particular. He may, perhaps, perceive something simple and continu'd, which he calls *himself*; tho' I am certain there is no such principle in me.

"But setting aside some metaphysicians of this kind, I may venture to affirm of the rest of mankind, that they are nothing but a bundle or collection of different perceptions, which succeed each other with an inconceivable rapidity, and are in a perpetual flux and movement."

David Hume, *A Treatise of Human Nature*

The hacker culture is neither good nor evil, but instead focuses on getting results. It is self-reliant and rooted in an anti-authoritarian embrace of individuality. No citizen is beholden to any single person, only to the quality of work being done.

Hacker ethics

ANDREW ZIMMERMAN JONES ON THE MORAL CODE OF THE GIRL WITH THE DRAGON TATTOO

Following some of Wikileaks's biggest successes, Julian Assange is at the epicentre of an international criminal investigation – accused of theft, espionage, aiding terrorists and sexual assault. He has responded by calling it a smear campaign conducted by governments he has exposed. Sound familiar? The editor-in-chief of *The New York Times* called Assange "The Boy Who Kicked the Hornet's Nest".

Most people use the term "hacker" to mean someone who breaks into a computer system in order to gain access to private information, but not everyone agrees. The hacker community tends to view hacking as a creative effort to overcome problems, both inside and outside the computing realm.

When Benjamin Franklin crafted the first bifocal lens, there's a sense in which he was hacking eyeglasses. Genetic manipulation is called "hacking the genome". A recent book entitled *Hack the Planet* describes technology's potential to remedy climate issues before they are irreparable, while *Astronomy Hacks: Tips and Tools for Observing the Night Sky* is a popular introductory book for budding stargazers.

There is even a sense in which hackers have a distinctive moral code. In his book *Hackers: Heroes of the Computer Revolution*, Stephen Levy was one of the first journalists to outline a "hacker ethic":

- Access to computers – and anything that might teach you something about the way the world works – should be unlimited and total.

Andrew Zimmerman Jones is author of *String Theory for Dummies* (John Wiley, 2009). This article is abridged from *The Girl with the Dragon Tattoo and Philosophy*, edited by **Eric Bronson**, and is part of a continuing series of extracts from the Blackwell Philosophy and Pop Culture series.

- All information should be free.
- Mistrust authority and promote decentralisation.
- Hackers should be judged by their hacking, not bogus criteria such as degrees, age, race or position.
- You can create art and beauty on a computer.
- Computers can change your life for the better.

In this short list, we begin to see some of the reasons why this culture appeals to Lisbeth Salander. The hacker culture is neither good nor evil, but instead focuses on getting results. It is self-reliant and rooted in an anti-authoritarian embrace of individuality. No citizen is beholden to any single person, only to the quality of work being done. It suits her personality well.

Ethics or not, the potentially destructive power of hacking has been clear for some time. In 1997, anthropology professor Steven Mizrach analysed hacker texts and proposed a new set of hacker ethics, including a concern over abuse, and a focus on privacy and social responsibility.

Lisbeth alludes to this stronger sense of social responsibility when she says, "I also have principles ... I call them *Salander's Principles*. One of them is that a bastard is always a bastard, and if I can hurt a bastard by digging up shit about him, then he deserves it." In a TEDGlobal interview, Assange identified similar motivations when describing the values at the core of his own work. "Capable, generous men do not create victims; they nurture victims."

Although Lisbeth has no problem busting heads in real life, her hacking emphasises stealth. She may implant secret programs that create mirror networks over the internet, but she doesn't create viruses for the sake of generating mayhem.

For example, when she trespasses in Armansky's computer, she says she just wanted to know what the company was up to, "to see the lay of the land".

Many young people do not think about ownership the same way their parents did. The digital revolution and the mainstreaming of hacker culture have resulted in a world where boundaries of ownership are rapidly changing. Tech-savvy youth download music and stream videos, never holding anything as prosaic as a CD or DVD in

Benjamin Franklin "hacked" eyeglasses

their hands. These new methods create all kind of questions of ownership, including how to apply copyright protections in the digital age.

This transformation in the way we view intellectual property is straight out of the hacker ethic. According to Steven Mizrach, "Stealing ... from a large institution like a corporation or government is OK. Stealing ... from an individual or small nonprofit is not ... Thus the new hacker ethic ... does not embrace theft; instead it simply defines certain things (like information) as not being personal property, or certain actions (using phone service) as 'borrowing' rather than theft."

Lisbeth clearly feels comfortable accessing information she wants at any time, prompting Blomkvist to say, "We need to have a talk on the subject of what's yours and what's mine."

Blomkvist isn't alone. Individuals want privacy, businesses want privacy, and governments want privacy. In his non-fiction book *The Transparent Society*, science fiction author David Brin explores the issue by distinguishing between ⋙

the lowdown/pop culture

97

Mistrust authority and promote decentralisation

privacy for individual citizens and privacy for "the mighty", which includes both corporations and governments. So where does one draw the line between the citizen and the mighty in the *Millennium* trilogy?

At the end of *The Girl with the Dragon Tattoo*, Blomkvist agrees to suppress the truth about Martin Vanger. Is this act in the interest of the personal privacy of Harriet Vanger, or the mighty interest of the Vanger Corporation? In this case, the secrecy serves both interests. It is Salander who lays things bare for Blomkvist:

"which is worse – the fact that Martin Vanger raped her out in the cabin or that you're going to do it in print?" Moments later, she extorts the Vanger Corporation to provide some form of social justice, in the form of money, for Martin's many victims and also for other abuse victims.

The situation is not nearly so easy for Blomkvist, because it straddles the two realms: the personal and the mighty. His ethical considerations include the belief that "Bastards too have a right to their private lives". But he also believes in reporting the truth, and a crime

had been committed that was worth reporting. "He who had lambasted his colleagues for not publishing the truth, here he sat, discussing, negotiating even, the most macabre cover-up he had ever heard of."

Although Blomkvist consents to the cover-up, it is clear that he still has reservations and as a journalist, the book's author, Stieg Larsson, may have experienced some tension over Blomkvist's decision himself. Indeed, this might be why he has Henrik Vanger offer Blomkvist's defence:

"You had to choose between your role as a journalist and your role as a human being. I could never have bought your silence. And I'm quite certain that you would have exposed us if Harriet had turned out in some way to have been implicated, or if you thought I was a cretin."

Salander, however, never had to make that choice. As a hacker, she followed her own set of principles and was able to hack a course of moral certainty out of the path that, for journalist Blomkvist, led to an ethical dilemma.

Zoom out and consider an analogous problem, not for individuals, but for society as a whole. David Brin begins an analysis of privacy with a description of two high-tech cities of the future that are free of crime, thanks to the ubiquitous placement of surveillance cameras. In one, the cameras report to a central police department, where the government maintains strict regulations on its citizens. In the other, any citizen may access any camera at any time. The technology is here, so the question he asks is: "Who will ultimately control the cameras?" Will it be the mighty or the citizens?

Brin argues in favour of putting the access and authority in the hands of the citizens to enforce accountability. If we try to keep it from individuals, then the corporations and governments will still find a way to get it. So it will be the individuals who lose out on their privacy. His conclusion is based on reasoning somewhat similar to the 2010 Supreme Court verdict in *Citizens United v. Federal Election Commission*. If we give the access and authority

Computers can change life for the better

to the individual, the corporations (and government) will have it by default as entities composed of individuals. No one loses out and most people gain.

Brin outlines a decentralised, transparent, Wikileaks-like approach to creating accountability. Eight years after Brin's book was published, Wikileaks was founded, throwing light into the dark corners of Brin's "mighty" while, at the same time, protecting the secrecy of their own sources, who Assange describes as classical whistleblowers. "Very rarely do we ever know [the source's identity]," he says, "and if we find out at some stage then we destroy that information as soon as possible."

This reflects the conflicting values in the hacker ethic and in Brin's society: personal privacy versus widespread openness in areas of public interest. Assange sees it too. He sees in society a conflict between the "enormous pressures to harmonise freedom of speech legislation and transparency legislation around the world … That's why it's a very interesting time to be in, because with just a little bit of effort, we can shift it one way or another."

Parmenides

by John Palmer

One thing that makes philosophy a uniquely dynamic discipline is its tendency to understand its own history in new ways, as the issues defining its present develop and shift. Our understanding of the figure who stands at the very beginning of western metaphysics – Parmenides of Elea – provides an excellent example of this phenomenon. Because Parmenides concerned himself abstractly with the metaphysics of being, he remains among the most difficult of philosophers to understand. Brace yourself for a little complexity.

Parmenides was active during the earlier half of the fifth century BCE in the Greek colonies of southern Italy. He composed a poem in epic hexameters, now only partially extant, describing a revelation received from the goddess Night. This revelation comprised a metaphysical demonstration of the nature of "true reality", a part of the poem that we possess virtually intact, and an elaborate and innovative account of the world's origins and workings, now mostly lost. The goddess began by describing two ways of

John Palmer is associate professor of philosophy at the University of Florida and author of *Parmenides and Presocratic Philosophy* (Oxford, 2009)

inquiry Parmenides might pursue in his search for genuine understanding: "the one, that it is and that it cannot not be, | is the path of conviction, for it attends upon true reality, | but the other, that it is not and that it must not be, | this, I tell you, is a path wholly without report: | for neither could you apprehend what is not, for it is not to be accomplished, | nor could you indicate it".

In the last two of these verses Bertrand Russell detected an anticipation of a problem with which he was deeply concerned, namely, how to understand the significance of negative existential statements, statements about things that don't actually exist. A generation of historians followed Russell's lead by developing comprehensive interpretations of Parmenides based upon ascribing to him the notion that one can only speak meaningfully of what is or exists. They explained the poem's metaphysical demonstration as an account of what, contrary to all appearances, actually exists. The goddess lists the attributes she will show true reality to have in the following verses: "What Is is ungenerated and deathless, | whole and uniform, and still and perfect". Parmenides was consequently understood as claiming that only one thing exists and that it is, despite all appearances, an ungenerated and imperishable, homogeneous, and invariant plenum – a single whole free from any and all change.

As philosophers in the latter part of the twentieth century became more interested in the metaphysics of necessity, it became apparent that the goddess's specifications of the two ways of inquiry specify two basic modalities or ways of being: necessary being and necessary non-being or impossibility. Since there can be no apprehension of what is not and must not be, the second way of inquiry is set aside immediately. (How, for example, could one know anything about something like a square circle, something that cannot

Gareth Southwell

possibly be?) The goddess subsequently introduces a third way of inquiry – "that it is and is not the same | and not the same"– that amounts to a specification of contingent or non-necessary being. Although she disparages the kind of understanding to be had of mutable and contingent entities, the goddess nevertheless provides Parmenides with a superior account of all such things in the cosmological portion of her revelation. That Parmenides is credited with being the first to maintain that the earth is round and with basing his cosmology on a plurality of basic stuffs are both indicative of its superiority.

On Parmenides' view, however, the highest order of understanding comes only from focusing one's thoughts on what must be. What the metaphysical demonstration of Parmenides' poem actually does, therefore, is deduce what an entity that is in this way has to be like just in virtue of its way of being. The attributes it is demonstrated to have amount to a set of temporal and spatial perfections: everlasting existence, immutability, the internal invariances of wholeness and uniformity, and the invariance at its extremity of being spherical or optimally shaped. What is and cannot not be thus proves to be not only a necessary but, in many ways, a perfect entity.

For much of the twentieth century Parmenides was associated with a paradoxical monism that denied existence to the familiar objects of experience. Proper appreciation of his pioneering concern with the metaphysics of modality now makes it possible to understand the magnitude of his achievement and his impact on thinkers from Plato to Anselm and beyond.

Parfit's mountain

JUSSI SUIKKANEN ON A LONG-AWAITED BOOK THAT COULD CHANGE OUR UNDERSTANDING OF MORALITY

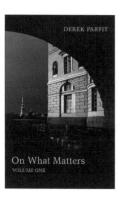

On What Matters, two-volume set by **Derek Parfit** (Oxford University Press) £30.00/$55.00 (hb)

For a long time, I have been sceptical about whether Derek Parfit's second treatise in moral philosophy will ever be published. I have often been told that Parfit is just about to submit the manuscript to his publisher, after which it will be quickly printed. The book has, however, so far failed to make its way to the shops. Experience has taught me to stop expecting it to appear.

During this time, Parfit's manuscript has nevertheless become a philosophical classic. Its title also changed from *Climbing the Mountain* to *On What Matters*. Parfit circulated several versions of the manuscript by email to large audiences, and the manuscript has even been openly available on the Internet. A large number of Anglo-American philosophy departments have organised reading groups on it, and I have even helped to organise a conference on the book and to publish the proceedings. The buzz created by Parfit's book has been phenomenal.

I am now finally beginning to believe that the manuscript will be published. The publisher was still unable to send me a review copy of the book for the purposes of this review, but they provided me with an electronic copy, which looks like the final typeset version.

So what is the book like in its final form? The first thing to notice is how the manuscript has grown from a few hundred to a whopping 1,365 pages. The publisher, Oxford University Press, should not only be given credit for their patience

Jussi Suikkanen is lecturer in philosophy at the University of Birmingham and co-editor, with John Cottingham, of *Essays on Derek Parfit's On What Matters* (Blackwell, 2009)

but also for keeping the price of the now two-volume set reasonable. Re-reading these volumes will, of course, now take months and studying them thoroughly will take years. The appropriate length for a review of these volumes would itself be a short book.

I can here only offer my first impressions of the final product. What strikes me most now is the philosophical method that Parfit employs again and again throughout the book. It is the oldest tool in the philosophers' kit. Parfit proceeds by attacking familiar versions of general ethical principles with innovative counter-examples. He then makes these principles more and more sophisticated until they survive the thought experiments.

Parfit is a master of this art. In the first volume, he focuses on the most basic general ethical principles such as the Golden Rule, Kant's formulations of the categorical imperative, and recent variations on contractualist and consequentialist principles. The counter-examples used to test and stretch these principles are brilliantly innovative. During this process, the simple Golden Rule that "we ought to treat others as we would want others to treat us" develops, for example, into the sophisticated thesis that "we ought to treat *everyone* as we would rationally be willing to be treated if we were going to be in all of these people's positions, and would be relevantly like them". Parfit's new formulations of the fundamental ethical principles will have a lasting impact on how the core of the main ethical theories will be understood in the future.

Parfit also has a "master argument". Its conclusion is that, when we understand the major ethical principles correctly, they all agree about which actions are permissible. This argument seems to work only if we understand some of the ethical principles as lacking substantial moral content (as we probably should anyway).

Unfortunately, Parfit applies his method also when he takes part in the debates about the nature of reasons, rationality, and free will, and especially in the metaethical debates about the nature of normative thought, language, properties and knowledge. Perhaps because of this, Parfit's work is less successful in these areas outside normative ethics. This shows that, as an area of intellectual investigation, metaethics differs from normative ethics in significant respects.

Metaethicists attempt to construct broad illuminative accounts about our practical engagement with the world by trying to combine elements of philosophy of mind and language, epistemology, metaphysics, ethics, and even psychology into all-encompassing, coherent, theoretical wholes. Even if there are always, of course, details to be given and technical problems to be solved, metaethicists try to build big pictures with explanatory power. Such theorising does not proceed by formulating succinct principles and testing them with counter-examples.

Parfit is a non-naturalist cognitivist. He thus thinks that there are distinct normative properties, and that we have true beliefs about them. Unfortunately, despite his best efforts, he still, even in the final version, fails to sufficiently illuminate the exact nature of these properties and say how we manage to talk and think about them. Furthermore, Parfit often fails to resist the temptation to understand the alternative views as not much more than short principles, which can be quoted from the writings of their defenders and easily dismissed with counter-examples. Because of this, Parfit's criticisms of the alternative metaethical views sometimes appear superficial.

review/what matters

103

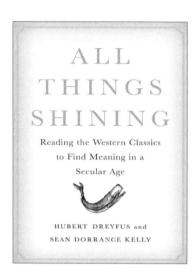

ALL THINGS SHINING

Reading the Western Classics to Find Meaning in a Secular Age

HUBERT DREYFUS and SEAN DORRANCE KELLY

Where the West went wrong

TROY JOLLIMORE SEEKS THE CURE FOR NIHILISM IN A GOOD CUP OF COFFEE

All Things Shining: Reading the Western Classics to Find Meaning in a Secular Age, by **Hubert Dreyfus** and **Sean Dorrance Kelly** (Free Press) £17.99/$26.00 (hb)

The work of a pair of esteemed and successful contemporary academic philosophers – Sean Kelly, chair of Harvard's philosophy department, and Hubert Dreyfus of UC Berkeley – *All Things Shining* is nevertheless a highly atypical book of philosophy. Unlike most philosophy books, *All Things Shining* tries to address existentially important topics and aspires to a general, non-specialist audience. It contains no logical formulas and no jargon. Its tone is informal, sometimes downright breezy. At times, it is even fun to read.

The book centres on a familiar theme: our time is a nihilistic one in which meaning and fulfilment are hard to come by. But *All Things*

Troy Jollimore is associate professor of philosophy at California State University, Chico. He is the author of *Love's Vision* (Princeton University Press, 2011) and two books of poetry.

Shining's aim is not only to bemoan or diagnose our spiritual ills, but to cure them. "The world used to be, in its various forms, a world of sacred, shining things. The shining things now seem far away. This book is intended to bring them close once more."

How do the authors intend to deliver on this ambitious promise? The subtitle might lead one to expect that the authors' recommendation will be to read more literature, that it is in the great books of the Western canon that we will find those elusive "shining things". In fact, with the exception of Homer and Melville, the two canonical authors whose masterpieces anchor *All Things Shining*'s historical account, the point of the book's extraordinarily and at times irritatingly compressed guided tour of Western thought is to show how and where Western thought went wrong: how the great thinkers of our tradition led us away from the Homeric paradise we once occupied and into the morally and spiritually bleak landscape of today.

Thus Augustine gets the blame for formulating Christianity in a way that "can't make sense of an embodied, incarnated Christ"; Dante misses the opportunity to correct this by choosing to emphasise an abstract deity over the tantalisingly concrete Beatrice; and, perhaps most destructively of all, Descartes' rationalism and focus on the inner self causes profound alienation, severing the natural connection to the world enjoyed by the ancient Greeks, who, because they understood themselves in terms of "public and shareable moods", were "open to the world in a way that we, who are skilled at introspection and who think of moods as private experiences, can barely comprehend".

The emphasis on individual autonomy that is Descartes' legacy (and Kant's) finds its contemporary manifestation in the novelist David Foster Wallace, the talented and successful novelist whose suicide symbolises contemporary despair. "[T]he sacred in Wallace – insofar as he can see such a phenomenon at all – is something *we impose* upon experience; there is nothing *given* about it at all." This is, again, in marked contrast to the ancient Greeks' attunement to external reality. As the authors summarise the point, "The modern view that we are entirely responsible for our existence stands in radical contrast with the Homeric idea that we act at our best when we open ourselves to being drawn from without."

How, then, can we get past the autonomy-grounded nihilism of the Descartes–Kant–Wallace tradition and re-achieve the Homeric Greeks' natural and spontaneous way of being-in-the-world? The authors' answer is complex, vague and a little disappointing. Partly it involves cultivating attitudes that have been systematically neglected in contemporary life: gratitude,

wonder and *eros*. Another part seems to involve being both realists and pluralists about value, by learning to reject scepticism and monotheism. We are to cease constantly searching for hidden meanings, and to accept superficial pleasures and apparently meaningful pursuits at face value. The kinds of knowledge and skill involved in serious dedication to a craft, for instance, are meaningful and value-laden in a way that seems inherently anti-nihilistic.

More surprisingly, perhaps, Dreyfus and Kelly claim that spectator sports can provide shared public experiences of communal ecstasy, which they unwisely insist on referring to as (ugh) "whooshing up". Even so minor a thing as a good cup of coffee, they suggest, can be full of meaning if one makes it into "a ritual rather than a routine, a meaningful celebration of oneself and one's environment rather than a generic and meaningless performance of a function".

Some readers will find such examples trivial to the point of parody, and will be unmoved by the idea that taking pleasure in "the joy of a crowd rising as one in the spontaneous celebration of a feat of human greatness, the cozy warmth of the fireside, [or] the comfort and gratitude of a family meal" could be the key to defeating nihilistic alienation. And some will be irritated by the casualness and, at times, shallowness of the book's history of Western thought. These complaints are not groundless. Still, we should appreciate Dreyfus and Kelly's original and intermittently provocative contribution to the conversation about meaning and value – even if, in the end, their way of dealing with our spiritual and intellectual woes is more or less to shrug their shoulders and ask, *So what was the problem again?*

review/religious law

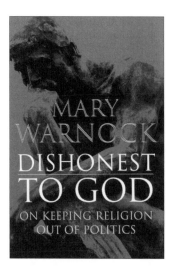

Politics, for God's sake

SCOTT AIKIN AND ROBERT TALISSE ASK WHETHER RELIGION SHOULD INFORM LAW

Dishonest to God: On Keeping Religion out of Politics by **Mary Warnock** (Continuum) £10.99/$16.95 (pb)

Mary Warnock pursues three objectives in this book. The first is to examine the difference between religious and moral reasons. The second is to argue that the authority of religion and law are dependent upon morality. The third is to demonstrate that, even though religion is disposable, religious traditions deserve respect from secularists.

Warnock's arguments are grounded in first-hand experiences with policymaking. Her extensive involvement in British politics supplies a range of stirring stories in which members of

Scott Aikin and Robert Talisse teach philosophy at Vanderbilt University. They are authors of *Reasonable Atheism: A Moral Case for Respectful Disbelief* (Prometheus, 2011).

parliament and barristers wrestle with issues regarding the value of human life. In one especially fascinating case, the demarcation between moral and religious reasons comes into question. In a 1967 debate in the House of Lords regarding abortion, the Earl of Longford avowed that "2,000 years of Christian tradition" is committed to the *sanctity* of human life. Warnock writes, "So was his argument based on religion or not? I think his repeated invocation of the concept of sanctity shows that ... his judgement was a religious judgement."

Warnock's point is that certain words invoke a religious viewpoint that must be distinguished from a naturalistic conception of value. She says, "The use of the word 'sacred' reinforces the religious background ... To describe something as 'sacred' is to invest it with an air of the supernatural, to give it a mysterious value above the value we may attach to the merely profane."

106

According to Warnock, moral value has no such supernatural source. Rather, it is the result of a combination of our sentiments and the fact of our sociability. Value is fully explicable within a naturalistic worldview. This conception of value ushers in the second phase of the book. Warnock argues that morality is prior to religion and law. This priority is a *dependency* relation; the authority of religious and legal rules derives from – and hence depends upon – the authority of morality. Accordingly, Warnock proposes a reconstruction of the supernatural overtones of religious terms. For example, she claims that when religious believers speak of the sanctity of human life, they mean to convey the view that "human life is enormously valuable and that causing death must never be lightly undertaken". In the case of law, Warnock observes that "moral principles give rise to [the] moral rights" that form the basis of legal judgments and rules.

Warnock then turns to the third phase of her book. If religion does not inform morality, then of what use is it? *Can* we (and *ought* we to) do without it? She writes, "Religion may not be necessary, but it can be good." She holds that the New Testament is a rich source of moral instruction; the ceremonies and rituals of worship are emotionally significant; and religion shapes many of our aesthetic ideals. She concludes: "there is no possible argument for holding that religion is outdated, or that it can be wholly replaced in society by science or any other imaginative enterprise."

Further, she argues against "militant atheists" who claim that "religion has done enormous harm", with the point that "it is not religion itself that is to blame", but rather "the belief that religion can provide unassailable moral truth and

... that it has the authority to enforce what its morality dictates". The political threat, then, is not religion *per se*, but rather the belief that religious truth carries with it political authority. According to Warnock, religion is perfectly acceptable, even welcome, in a democratic society, once believers recognise that the authority of their religious beliefs is at best *derivative*, parasitic upon the authority of secular morality.

The authority of religious and legal rules depends upon morality

Perhaps Warnock is right to defend religion in this sense. However, one must wonder whether religious belief so described is *religious* at all. It's easy to imagine a religious believer objecting that a belief with merely derivative authority is not properly religious. For many, religious belief is essentially of ultimate, all-encompassing authority. And sometimes the demands of that authority oppose the dictates of secular morality.

Dishonest to God is well worth reading. However, it seems that, at best, Warnock has made a case for welcoming in civil society a variety of religious belief that is liberal, tolerant, open-minded and democratic. We would not have thought that the civic *bona fides* of *that* kind of religious belief needed defending. More traditional forms of religious belief see religious authority as ultimate and non-derivative; hence they are more difficult to reconcile with modern democracy. One is left to wonder what role, if any, these more traditional views should play in our politics.

Morality on the brain

NEIL LEVY PRAISES PATRICIA CHURCHLAND'S HUMANISM

Braintrust: What Neuroscience Tells us about Morality by **Patricia Churchland** (Princeton University Press) £19.95/$24.95 (hb)

Neil Levy is head of neuroethics at the Florey Neuroscience Institute. He is the editor of the journal *Neuroethics* and author of *Hard Luck: How Luck Undermines Free Will and Moral Responsibility* (Oxford University Press, forthcoming).

I n some quarters, the Churchlands – Patricia and Paul – are notorious. They are the favourite demons for certain philosophers of mind because they advocate eliminative materialism: the view that our ordinary psychological language, with its talk of beliefs, desires, wishes, hopes and so on, is deeply flawed. For many of their opponents, the Churchlands' advocacy of a naturalistic successor for ordinary psychological talk smacks of scientism: the inappropriate extension of the methods and categories of science to areas of human experience that cannot properly be understood in these terms.

Eliminativism is not a topic that Patricia Churchland discusses in *Braintrust*, but her thoroughly naturalistic treatment of morality may – at any rate, *should* – help the critics to see that the threat of scientism may not be as great as they feared. The account of the nature and origins of morality that Churchland sketches here is thoroughly naturalistic and thoroughly grounded in the sciences. But it is also humanistic; indeed, it is a more humanistic vision than the one advanced by many of her opponents. For her, although the capacities that make us moral are the products of evolution and can be explained in detail by neuroscience, the content of morality is very importantly the product of human culture. It is not because of an about-face that her account is so thoroughly humanistic; it is because this is the picture that science actually supports.

Crudely, the picture Churchland sketches is this. In the very distant evolutionary past, organisms developed self-regulatory mechanisms designed to protect them against damage and ensure survival: mechanisms for damage detection such as pain, mechanisms for detection of adverse conditions such as the capacity to feel cold, and so on. These mechanisms together bring the animal to value its own well-being, where well-being is understood as a set of internal states being maintained within a certain range. This self-valuing is the origin of all values, moral values included.

A crucial step in the development of morality occurred with the extension of valuing beyond the organism. Self-valuing mechanisms developed, of course, because they were adaptive: they played a pivotal role in the survival of the organism. For precisely the same reason, these mechanisms tended to extend their range, so that offspring, at least when young, were included within their ambit. Animals come to value the survival of their offspring in much the same kind of way they value themselves. Some analogue of this kind of valuing gradually came to be extended to other relatives and to other members of the small groups within which our ancestors lived.

So far the picture sketched applies as much to other social animals as it does to human beings. But human social organisation and human morality are plausibly much more complex than the morality of other animals. The next step in the development of morality is one that has probably only been taken by human beings, and it is at this point that culture enters the picture. For relations of trust to extend much beyond the circle of kith and kin, human social organisation had to change. Trade between groups establishes norms of cooperation and mechanisms for their enforcement; social conventions signal conformity to a code and make behaviour more predictable. These norms and conventions may differ across regions. Although the mechanisms that drive moral norms are universal, the content of morality is very significantly local. Churchland thus rejects currently popular views according to which most of the content of morality is innate.

The view is humanistic inasmuch as it emphasises the centrality of culture to the content of human morality. It is also humanistic in its emphasis on moral deliberation as a set of uncodifiable skills. Moral decision-making – like almost all decision-making in the messy real world – is a *constraint satisfaction process*, not a matter of following rules. When we make decisions, we try to find a solution that best balances a range of competing considerations, Churchland argues. This entails that although there are better and worse solutions to problems, many problems do not have a uniquely rational solution. Against those philosophers who have sought to codify morality exhaustively, Churchland argues that there are no significant rules that are truly exceptionless. The picture of moral reasoning as a practical skill she paints here is, as she recognises, strongly reminiscent of the approach advocated by Aristotle in ancient Greece and by Confucius around the same time. Contemporary science might threaten our received view of the mind in some ways, then, but in others it supports it. It vindicates the main lessons of one of the most ancient moral views, a view that remains vibrant and that is strongly rooted in common sense. The vision of human morality that emerges from *Braintrust* is rooted in the sciences, which Churchland copiously cites and elaborates. But the vision is nevertheless one that celebrates those capacities that poets and philosophers have celebrated as distinctively human.

review/neuroethics

109

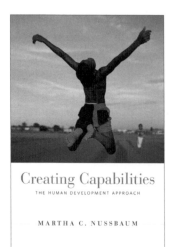

Creating Capabilities
THE HUMAN DEVELOPMENT APPROACH

MARTHA C. NUSSBAUM

A new approach

THOM BROOKS RECOMMENDS AN ACCESSIBLE BOOK ABOUT CAPABILITIES

Creating Capabilities: The Human Development Approach by **Martha C Nussbaum** (Belknap/Harvard University Press) £16.96,$22.95 (hb)

The capabilities approach has attracted increasing attention in recent years. It is easy to see why. The approach is compelling, and there are many areas where it has yet to be applied. There's also no lack of outstanding major contributions to how the approach might inform particular policy areas, such as development. However, there has been a real need for a more introductory work that makes clear its aims and ambitions, in order to help further broaden its appeal. *Creating Capabilities* fills this need beautifully. And we are guided through this major restatement by one of the main architects of the capabilities approach. This is a book not to be missed.

Thom Brooks is reader in political and legal philosophy at Newcastle University and author of *Global Justice: An Introduction* (Wiley-Blackwell, forthcoming)

Nussbaum begins with Vasanti, whose story offers a useful narrative by which the capabilities approach is explained and defended. Vasanti lives in India. She was married to a gambler and alcoholic who was abusive towards her and eventually they divorced. Although she worked for a time, she remained dependent on her family, until she came into contact with the Self-Employed Women's Organization, an NGO that assists poor women. This organization provides women like Vasanti with access to education, healthcare and even microcredit.

Nussbaum asks: "What theoretical approach could direct attention to the most significant features of Vasanti's situation, promote an adequate analysis of it, and make pertinent recommendations for action?" Her argument is that the capabilities approach does best where others fail.

For example, the standard approach would focus on Gross Domestic Product (GDP) per capita: the higher the GDP, the more "developed" a region or state is. This approach is a poor indicator for thinking about development. One reason is that the GDP per capita is an average. South Africa during apartheid often scored highly on GDP per capita, but this was because great wealth was concentrated in too few hands. A high GDP might indicate (measurable) wealth, but it offers no evidence that this wealth has reached those who need it most.

It is also too crude. Our understanding should move away from considerations of resources only, because having more resources does not indicate greater well-being. The citizens of Kerala illustrate this well. They have fewer resources than those in more advanced regions, but they score rather highly on literacy rates, equality and longevity. Moreover, equal resources do not necessarily entail equal treatment: some people require more resources than others. Wheelchair users may require ramps to access buildings, and these ramps may be more expensive than alternatives. Installing ramps does not entail favouring one group over another, but it does mean all groups are treated equally.

This equal treatment is with respect to their shared dignity and freedom of choice. It is these features that best set Nussbaum's capabilities approach apart from alternatives. It is a pluralistic theory of justice, open to revision, with the aim of respecting dignity and choice. A common illustration is fasting. A person who fasts has something in common with another who is starving: both are deprived of food and nutrients. The difference is that the fasting person has a choice, and the starving person does not. We should ensure that our political institutions are built around preserving our capabilities to choose in various areas.

The list of these areas has not changed in Nussbaum's various formulations in recent years. It includes choices with regard to life; bodily health; bodily integrity; senses, imagination and thought; emotions; practical reason; affiliation; concern for other species; play; and control over

Having resources does not indicate well-being

one's environment (both political and material). The just society is one where all may freely exercise capabilities in these areas if and when they so choose. The capabilities list is also deliberately vague without lacking content. This is in order to allow for easier application across cultural and other differences. The capabilities approach can speak to the particular narratives we find in cases such as Vasanti: the approach can speak on areas and issues where other approaches fall silent.

There is much more that can be said about the detail of Nussbaum's new restatement, and why I believe it is so compelling. Some will worry about whether our theories may amount to some ill-formed cultural imperialism. This is certainly not the case here, as cross-cultural examples abound, and this is a real strength of the book. Nussbaum makes the capabilities approach genuinely come alive with vivid illustrations and beautifully crafted arguments.

Creating Capabilities is an outstanding achievement of political philosophy that will open readers to the excitement of the capabilities approach. I cannot recommend it highly enough.

review/capabilities

111

Freedom fighters

DANA NELKIN AND SAM RICKLESS WONDER HOW A TEXT MESSAGE COULD COMPROMISE FREE WILL

The Adjustment Bureau is loosely based on a story by **Philip K Dick** and directed by **George Nolfi**

*T*he Adjustment Bureau is a thriller built around a romance that ends with a moral about the importance of exercising free will in determining one's future. David Norris (Matt Damon) is an unattached, up-and-coming Brooklyn congressman who meets Elise Sellas (Emily Blunt), an unattached, up-and-coming ballet dancer, as he prepares to give a concession speech ending his bid to become a US senator. David, who is smitten, learns no more than Elise's first name before they part. The speech then positions David for another run at the same seat. Soon after his electoral loss, David meets Elise again, and the second meeting rekindles their feelings for one another. But although the first meeting was supposed to happen, the second meeting was not.

It turns out that the world is governed according to a seemingly beneficent master plan, run by The Chairman (God?), and implemented by an Adjustment Bureau composed of hundreds of male (why male?), possibly angelic employees, who dress like FBI agents from the 1960s. They sport fedoras that somehow give them the power to move instantaneously between non-contiguous places through carefully placed doors all over New York City. As David quickly learns, the adjusters are busy arranging things to make him win the next election and eventually become president. But there's a catch: the adjusters tell David that he will not fulfil the master plan if he chooses to pursue his budding relationship with Elise. This sets up the conflict at the heart of the film: David will do whatever he can to find Elise

Dana Nelkin and **Sam Rickless** are professors of philosophy at the University of California, San Diego

and win her affections, while the adjusters (with one notable exception) will do whatever they can to keep David and Elise apart.

The central philosophical theme of the film concerns free will. Here the film fails to provide determinate answers to important questions, and in some cases the answers it does provide border on incoherence. At a critical moment, David is led to believe that it follows from the adjusters' interventions that no human being has free will. But this claim is in tension with other assumptions at the heart of the plot.

The first assumption is that the bureau has limited manpower, and so focuses on human decisions with important ramifications. This suggests that, despite the best efforts of the bureau, most humans are free with respect to many of their actions and decisions. The second assumption is that adjusters have three kinds of supernatural powers, and one notable limitation: the ability to cause situational changes (such as text messages and coffee spills); the ability to replace a person's memories; and the ability to alter reasoning; but they can't alter someone's personality or emotions.

There are problems related to the second assumption. One is that the ability to change a person's reasoning may well entail the very power to alter personality or emotions that the film precludes. Another is that it is arguably a mistake to suppose that either the ability to cause situational changes or its exercise threatens free will; even if adjusters are manipulating circumstances in the service of a hidden plan, it does not follow (although it may seem to at first blush) that human decisions are unfree. For example, the fact that David's campaign manager receives an urgent text message at a key moment in the film as the result of an adjustment doesn't remove David's free will any more than does his receiving a text message from another human being simply trying to reach him.

What may be a flaw in the film – the failure to convey a thought-out and consistent view about what free will is or about what constitute genuine threats to it – can also provide an oppor-

It follows from the adjusters' interventions that no human being has free will

tunity to raise interesting philosophical questions. Is the existence of a master plan itself, perhaps combined with adjusters *prepared*, if necessary, to intervene, sufficient to remove free will? Or if only actual interventions preclude free will, do these include making situational changes such as bumping people carrying coffee, as well as direct interference in a person's reasoning by passing a special wand over his head before an important meeting?

Of course, the lead adjuster's claim that humans have no free will may well be mistaken. Indeed, the end of the film suggests, cleverly, that it may be part of the Chairman's master plan to mislead his own adjusters, and give David the opportunity to exercise his freedom, even in the face of his mistaken belief that such exercise would be either impossible or ineffective. David's choice is predictable and that predictability detracts from the suspense the film tries to create. But the plot twist based on the possibility that deception of his own adjusters is part of the Chairman's master plan is curiously satisfying.

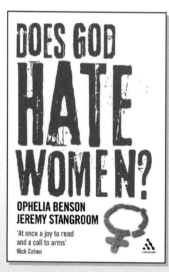

Q & A

THE FOUNDER OF VIRTUE EPISTEMOLOGY
ON WHAT IT REALLY TAKES TO KNOW

Knowing Full Well begins with problems owed to Plato but shaped recently by Gettier. Could you say what the problems are?

In his *Theaetetus* Plato inquires into the nature of knowledge, in the *Meno* also into its value. In contemporary epistemology, both problems have occupied centre stage. A belief can fall short of knowledge despite being true, if for example it derives from trust in a liar who happens on that occasion to tell the truth. Even a competently formed true belief might still fall short, since you might have excellent reason to trust the liar, who has kept his deceitful character well hidden.

In order to constitute knowledge, a belief must satisfy some condition beyond being a belief and being true. If knowledge that p is always, necessarily better than true belief that falls short of knowledge, then the additional condition must import some normatively positive content. When one ponders a question, it would always be better to answer knowledgeably than to answer correctly but just by luck. As we have seen with the help of our liar, moreover, this further condition cannot amount simply to the belief's being competently formed.

True belief about the location of Larissa will get you there just as well as knowledge. So, why should we think that knowledge would always exceed in value a corresponding merely true belief? What further value is imported, if it does not help you reach your destination?

Roughly, how does your approach to knowledge solve these problems?

I propose an account of human knowledge in terms of performance normativity. This is a normativity constitutive of knowledge, which ⋙

Knowing Full Well by **Ernest Sosa** is published by Princeton University Press at £20.95, $29.95 (hb)

review/q&a

explains its special value. On this account, a belief aimed at truth is a cognitive performance, and is to be assessed in the way of such performances generally. Its value is the value of a performance whose success manifests the performer's competence. That is the nature of our most basic knowledge, and it also explains the special value of such knowledge. Knowledge is always "better" than would be the corresponding merely true belief because performance whose success manifests the performer's competence is always thus "better" than performance whose success does not manifest such competence, either because it does not succeed, or because it succeeds through luck as opposed to competence.

What does it mean to say that a belief is apt?

I focus on performances aimed at a certain outcome, as when an archer aims his shot at a target. His shot can then be assessed in three respects: (i) Is it accurate? Does it hit the target? (ii) How adroit is it, how skilful? (iii) Does its accuracy manifest its adroitness or is it accurate merely through luck? A shot might hit the target and might be highly skilful, yet it hits the target only after an initial gust takes it off course, and a second gust puts it back on course. The accuracy of that shot does not manifest the adroitness of the archer. Its accuracy is due rather to the lucky second gust. The shot is accurate and adroit, but fails to be apt.

How do we derive knowledge from things like calculators and thermometers, and from testimony? Is there a difference between those instruments and our eyes and ears?

Some of our justification for trusting instruments has an inductive basis, but much of it derives also from testimony. And the testifier must be able through his utterances to deliver safe deliverances about what he thinks on the topic at hand. These must be deliverances that would not be delivered unless their content (concerning what the speaker thinks) were true. Testimonial knowledge thus presupposes instrumental knowledge through the instrument of language, and it is out of the question to reduce *all* instrumental knowledge to testimonial knowledge.

The instruments on which we depend most extensively and fundamentally are the perceptual modules included in our native endowment. Much perceptual knowledge can thus be seen as instrumental. If our perceptual modules are reliable, we gain knowledge and epistemic justification by accepting their safe deliverances at face value.

Epistemically justified trust in our sensory sources is a gift of natural evolution, which provides us with perceptual modules that encapsulate sensory propositional content and reliability in a single package. We accept their deliverances at face value as a default stance, properly so. Our sensory states have their content in virtue of the fact that they normally respond to the truth of such content. They are thus apt for normally mediating between the relevant environmental facts suitable for such sensory uptake and the beliefs they tend to prompt.

Our senses are thus distinguished epistemically from ordinary instruments. We *can* have reasons for trusting our senses as we do, a trust justifiably based on these reasons. What is distinctive of our senses as epistemic instruments is that we do not *need*, and cannot have, sufficient reason for trusting each, with absolutely no reliance, either now or earlier, on any of the others.

Jean Kazez
imagine that

Animal husbandry

After a dry-spell of about two years, I am finally in love … with a novel. *The Evolution of Bruno Littlemore,* by Benjamin Hale (Twelve Books), is the autobiography of an upwardly mobile chimpanzee. Bruno recounts his life story to Gwen, an intern at the Zastrow Primate Research Center in Georgia, while reclining on a couch and sipping a glass of iced tea. A seasoned ape of twenty-four, he's bipedal, hairless, and loquacious. He's an actor, an artist, and an astute observer of the human condition; and he's more-or-less a murderer (as we learn on page one).

Bruno begins his memoirs with the earliest sign that he is atypical. "I never felt like I quite belonged to the same species as my mother or Céleste." That's Céleste his cage-mate at the Lincoln Park Zoo. "I loved Céleste, but I did not lust after her. I did not lust after her because she was a chimp. My erotic desires lay elsewhere, yes, even then."

Bruno desires women – human women. Daily they "sashay in their anthropic glory" past his quarters at the Lincoln Park Zoo. Then, when he is six, primatologist Lydia Littlemore enters his life. Entranced by her long blonde hair, intoxicated by her smell, and happy in her arms, off he goes to a behavioural psychology laboratory at the University of Chicago, where he stuns the scientists with his cognitive and linguistic skills.

Soon Bruno is living with Lydia, occupying the room that once belonged to her infant son, now dead. He learns to understand English, then learns to speak, and falls in love with one facet of human existence after another. He adores his new room. "My room! My, my, my, *my* room! Mine! My *area*! My *space*! (Do you realize what a godly luxury is the first-person possessive pronoun applied to physical space?)" He loves books and music, and he loves a TV show called *Francis the Gnome*; he loves the smell of women and watching them put on stockings; he loves Van Gogh (he starts painting himself) and department store mannequins.

The world of humans contains so many delights, but strange and terrifying things too. Bruno overhears Lydia and friend Tal Gozani (she of the terrifying puppet collection) discussing Noam Chomsky's view that non-human primates have no real capacity for language and starts regularly dreaming about a creepy, sinister, sallow creature – "the Gnome Chompy". In one of his dreams, "it was as if there was cement hardening ⋙

Jean Kazez teaches philosophy at Southern Methodist University in Dallas and is the author of *Animalkind: What We Owe to Animals* (Wiley-Blackwell, 2010)

in my throat. I could not even move my hand to point. The Gnome Chompy had robbed me of all my powers of communication." Bruno is horrified and fascinated by the way humans insist on a clear, impermeable line separating the human species and every other.

It turns out that Lydia is not just flexible about gender (Tal becomes a lover), but flexible about species. Bruno and Lydia fall deeply in love. Their love life gets off to a rough start (human bedroom rules and manners are tricky), but Bruno's lust for Lydia is matched by Lydia's for him. Noooooooooo! Yes. But don't call it bestiality (Bruno explains). Bestiality is what Bruno's father does to a frog at the beginning of the novel, with bad results for the frog. Our big reaction to inter-species sex (laugh, gasp, scream), even if both partners are essentially human, reveals a great deal about the deep importance we attach to species boundaries. (Peter Singer's infamous essay "Heavy Petting" says more about that topic.)

Not only is Bruno outwardly an ape, but when the love affair begins, he's still drinking from a sippy-cup and watching Sesame Street. He's two feet shorter than Lydia. But never mind – they are in love, and the sex is abundant and fantastic, we are reminded over and over again. (What's with Lydia? We never really find out.) Then there's trouble (how could it be otherwise?). There's a murder and a flight – as we know there will be on the first page – and many other adventures (perhaps a few too many).

Bruno is a lucky ape who constantly finds himself in the company of supportive, open-minded humans. But he also encounters his share of misfortune. Although a passionate humanist, and conversely, something of a speciesist – he finds his fellow apes pretty idiotic and

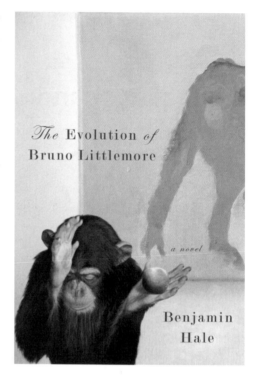

gross – he's also an advocate for animals. He demands his due, as an ape, and fair treatment for more strictly simian apes than he.

How can the human/animal boundary be seriously explored in the autobiography of such an unreal animal? It can, because Bruno's journey to full humanity illuminates what full humanity comprises. And also because Bruno is a philosophical ape, given to wonderfully engaging rumination about a vast array of subjects. The most striking thing about this novel is Bruno's charming, captivating, immensely entertaining voice. Over the novel's nearly 600 pages, he became so real to me that I can just about imagine that he's still at the Zastrow Research Center, rehearsing for his next theatrical performance, or working on a second set of memoirs, or seducing Gwen – but probably all three.

New bibles and unloved animals

A ROUNDUP OF REVIEWS OF
GOOD BOOKS AND SHRIVELLED RAISINS

Whatever else it might be, the Bible is almost certainly the best-selling book of all time. Or perhaps it's better to say that it's the most printed book, as many millions of copies are given away for free. By some estimates, a staggering 6 billion copies have been produced. No secular or non-religious volume comes anywhere close. Even Chairman Mao's *Little Red Book*, once required reading for a billion Chinese people, is left in the dust of Exodus.

Atheists and agnostics might therefore be cheered to learn that a secular contender has appeared. A C Grayling offers us *The Good Book: A Secular Bible*. According to the publisher, the book brings together "the wisdom of 2,500 years of contemplative non-religious writing on all that it means to be human – from the origins of the universe to small matters of courtesy and kindness in everyday life".

"It will be fascinating to see if *The*

The Good Book: A Secular Bible by **A C Grayling** (UK: Bloomsbury, US: Walker) £25, $35 (hb)

Good Book catches on", Michale Glitz writes for *Huffington Post Books*. "Maybe agnostics and atheists will embrace it; maybe Christians will embrace it too as a valuable collection of insights … I suppose some might be offended by *The Good Book* but they needn't be. You don't have to be a nonbeliever to find solace and wisdom in the distilled ideas presented here. It's a testament to the enduring power of the Bible that Grayling sought to draw upon its very form and structure."

I'm not entirely sure that it's testament to the power of Testament that Grayling had in mind when he included a secular version of God's commands. As Glitz reports, "Grayling does come up with his own Ten Commandments … 'Love well, seek the good in all things, harm no others, think for yourself, take responsibility, respect nature, do your utmost, be informed, be kind, be courageous: at least, sincerely try.'" Glitz asks, "Would any person of faith object to them?"

Quite possibly. Thus David Sexton in the *London Evening Standard*: "It's the Boy Scouts code: dib! dib! dib!, dob! dob! dob! – apart, that is, from that pathetic, HR termination, 'at least, sincerely try'. *The Good Book* is a colossal own goal. Nothing could show more plainly that there is a gigantic Bible-shaped hole in the lives of atheists, not so easily filled by one prize ass." ⊳⊳⊳

Perhaps it's only human nature to vent spleen when something that you find precious is set aside by others. If you are curious about the hidden mechanisms behind such reactions, this and more is the subject of David Brooks's *The Social Animal: the Hidden Sources of Love, Character and Achievement*. Brooks argues that there are two levels of the mind, a conscious bit and an unconscious bit, and the latter has a lot more to do with human action and success in life than the former. The book bounces back and forth between being a novel that tells the life stories of upwardly mobile yuppies Harold and Erica, and explaining what's really going on with them cognitively via repeated forays into the various sciences of human behaviour.

The idea that we are actuated by something other than conscious thought is, Thomas Nagel points out in *The New York Times*, not exactly news. "The importance and legitimacy of sentiment and social influence in determining human conduct was emphasized by figures of the British Enlightenment, notably David Hume, Adam Smith and Edmund Burke. Hume denied the dominance of reason, though he also offered brilliant analyses of the complex and systematic ways in which our sentiments, or passions, operate."

The real interest lies in what we do with this knowledge. "[E]ven if empirical methods enable us to understand subrational processes better," Nagel says, "the crucial question is, How are we to use this kind of self-understanding? Brooks emphasizes the ways in which it can improve our prediction and control of what people will do, but I am asking something different. When we discover an unacknowledged influence on our conduct, what should be our critical response? About this question Brooks has essentially nothing to say."

P Z Myers, reviewing the book for Salon.com, is considerably less charitable. "I don't even necessarily disagree with the biological and psychological studies sprinkled in short, pithy summaries like shrivelled little raisins of evidence in the gloppy porridge of his story; it's that they're just laid out so superficially and so discretely. … It's a collection of factlets."

He concludes, "I don't know whom this book is really written for. It's definitely not going to satisfy any scientists, or even any informed people who want to know more about how the brain works – there's no technical meat on the bones of this farce. It's certainly not going to satisfy anyone hoping for literary quality, or beauty and poetry, or even a good story. I suspect that its only virtue is in uniting C P Snow's two cultures, both of which will be populated with peeved readers flinging the book with great force across rooms everywhere."

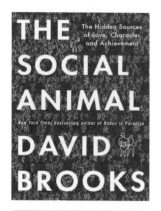

The Social Animal: the Hidden Sources of Love, Character and Achievement by **David Brooks** (Random House) $27 (hb) £14.99 (pb)

review/round-up

MY PHILOSOPHY

"His hypothesis is that if you take dope you're going to end up taking smack, but he'd actually got an incorrect application of Bayes' theorem ... the gateway theory, all obviously complete bollocks, based on a professor's ineptitude in statistics."

Britain's best-loved dope dealer

HOWARD MARKS TELLS JULIAN BAGGINI ABOUT PRISON, POT AND HEMPEL'S PARADOX

Academic philosopher or international drug smuggler? It's not a career choice many people find themselves having to make, but then Howard Marks has been in innumerable situations most of us can hardly imagine. Having opted to take the criminal route, Marks went on to become Britain's best known, and most-loved, dope dealer.

It's not surprising that his earlier forays into philosophy are overlooked in favour of the colourful story of life as a crook. Only ever dealing with marijuana, never "hard" drugs, Marks was involved with multi-million-dollar smuggling operations that brought him into contact with the likes of the IRA, MI6 and the Mafia. He was caught on several occasions, once being extradited from Spain to the USA where he served seven years in an Indiana prison. Once released, he published a best-selling autobiography, *Mr Nice*, which turned him into a cult figure. Since 1997, he has regularly performed live shows, in which he recounts tales of his life as an outlaw in his distinctive, gently lilting Welsh accent.

It's all a far cry from life in Oxford's Balliol College in the late sixties, when, as a physics undergraduate, Marks first came across philosophy, ▷▷▷

Julian Baggini is editor-in-chief of *tpm* and author of *The Ego Trick: What Does it Mean to be You?* (Granta, 2011)

121

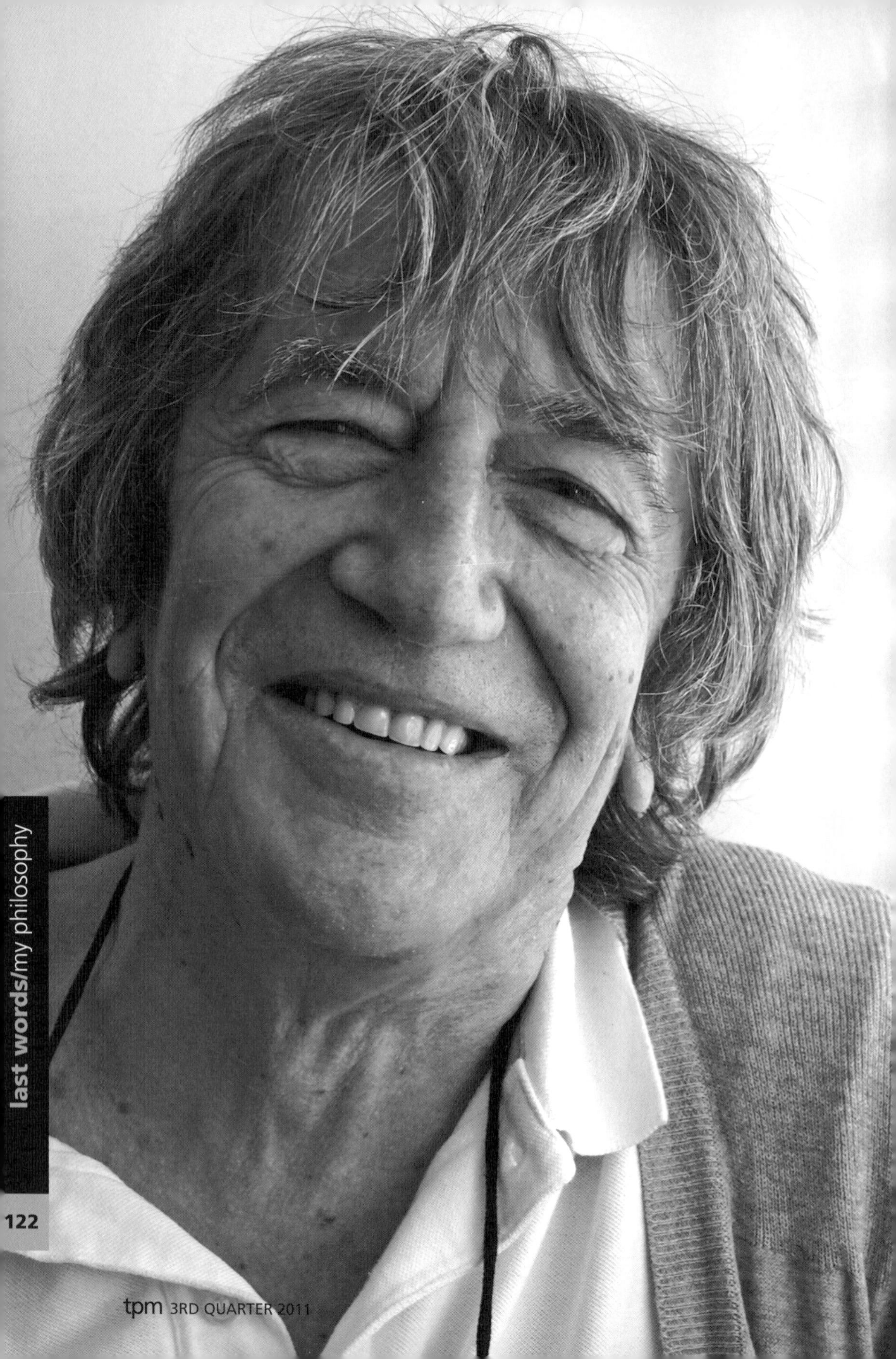

through friends who were studying it. "The people who were philosophers seemed to be a much more interesting bunch than the people who were nuclear physicists," Marks told me when I met him at London's Groucho Club, the favourite private club for movers and shakers in media and entertainment. He was persuaded by the philosopher and Balliol's admissions tutor Alan Montefiore to have a go at philosophy by writing an essay on the definition of good. This, Marks found, "was very, very complicated, not what I was hoping for at all. I discovered that it was much, much harder than I realised, and I switched back to physics."

"What was most inhibiting was the idea of coming up with anything new or novel. There was just so much written about moral philosophy that it seemed an impossible task to come up with anything original. Great minds have set themselves to it for millennia. Obviously I'm not going to contribute a fucking thing to this."

"It was a case of bad luck. Had it been something like the existence of space and time, I would have been much more at home with it." Indeed, his interest in philosophy did not go away, which is why he went on to take the one-year postgraduate History and Philosophy of Science diploma at Oxford, over 1968–69.

Marks had been spurred on to do this by his reading of Bertrand Russell's *History of Western Philosophy* while he was doing a postgraduate teacher training course. "I would still recommend it to anyone as the best book of philosophy that's ever been written, and Russell's probably one of the best philosophers that's ever been," says Marks. Russell taught him, in *The Problems of Philosophy,* "that philosophy isn't around to provide any answers. It's just a matter of framing the right questions. I liked that angle as well."

Because of his mathematical abilities, Marks found Russell's "eloquent" writing about logic compelling, and was grabbed by some of the paradoxes he discusses, particularly Hempel's, which shows that, in strict logical terms, the statement "All ravens are black" is equivalent to "Everything that is not black is not a raven." This became the subject of his postgraduate thesis.

"I became a personal friend of Freddy Ayer"

The world of Oxford philosophy in the late sixties was very easy-going, and Marks loved it. "It was great. I did feel very privileged very early on to be sharing spaces with brilliant minds. I became a personal friend of Freddy [A J] Ayer, for example. We just hit it off personally and he would drop round occasionally to my rooms and have a chat." If you read Ayer's autobiography, *A Part of My life,* after *Mr Nice,* you'd never have guessed this. Ayer's life story is told with an almost autistic detachment, while Marks is clearly an impulsive hedonist. So is there a side of Ayer he just didn't show, or a side of Marks that people don't know about. "Probably a bit of both. He was a big Tottenham Hotspur supporter, and I just thought that was incongruous that he would be going to a football match every Saturday. And I suppose my interest in philosophy is totally inappropriate to my career too. It's more just seeing the human side of him that he never seemed to express."

Marks also got to know Michael Dummett. On one occasion Marks missed a tutorial because he was in court speaking on behalf of someone who had been arrested on a demonstration against ⊳⊳⊳

Enoch Powell, the Conservative MP whose notorious "rivers of blood" speech inflamed anti-immigration feeling. Marks felt less guilty about playing hooky, however, when he discovered that Dummett was also there, speaking for another arrested demonstrator. "It's a wonderful combination: the right morals, a brilliant mind and someone who smokes himself to death. I found that very comforting."

There was, however, one connection between philosophy and his future career. Marks claims that, although he found doing physics more difficult when stoned, at least some philosophy was easier when high. "Philosophy is about finding counter-examples and I found it easier to find a counter example to any so-called true statement that anyone would make, and one that would be deemed original."

Marks thinks this has something to do with the fact that "The nature of cannabis is that it manifests itself as time seeming to slow down. I reason that there's only one possible explanation for that which is that one is thinking quicker."

Sceptics would say that people may think they are more profound when stoned, but they're just engaged in "bull-sessions", the facileness of which becomes evident in retrospect. "Yes, I think that happens too," agrees Marks. "But I notice, even with my writing these days, I know my writing's better when I'm stoned. There's no question about it. I look at it when I'm stoned, I look at it when I'm on coke, I look at it when I'm straight, I look at it when I'm pissed, it's undoubtedly better when I'm stoned. Far more tangents present themselves and therefore more interest."

Following the diploma, Marks got a place at Sussex University to study philosophy of science. At that point, an academic career looked like a real possibility. "No other career occurred to me other than smuggling or dealing, which was the only other competitor." But was he really attracted to it or was it just the only thing that seemed open? "The latter. I quite liked the comfort of an academic career. I quite liked not having to do much in the real world, the inexhaustible number of topics an academic can deal with, whereas if you're not an academic it's quite a humdrum list of things you have to deal with. Plus I quite liked the romance of the old rooms and the library. Socially it would be fine: lots of short terms of sitting around pontificating."

However, Sussex proved to be a great disappointment. "It didn't have the feeling of noble halls of learning and all that sort of thing. Everything from the rooms to the people, I just didn't like it." That extended to his tutor, the Polish logician Jerzy Giedymin: "a brilliant guy but so fucking boring". He was there just a year and quit. "And that was it really. Until I got nicked."

That is the curious fact about what Marks describes in his autobiography as his "sincere and lasting interest in the history and philosophy of science." He did come back to it, "but only when I was in prison. Each time I was busted and it looked like I'd be down there for a while, then I would immediately think, now's the time to go back to it and study it again, because there's little else to do. I don't read anything about it now. All that I've talked about is purely from memory from the old days. This is the longest in my life when I've not been in prison. You've caught me at my philosophical worst."

This is perhaps one of the most surprising arguments for the virtues of prison. "The same is true of yoga and physical fitness. I only do that

when I'm in prison. It's debauchery completely otherwise."

Indeed, Marks thinks incarceration did him a lot of good. "I think in my case I certainly emerged from prison a better person than when I went in there. Stronger moral fibre, less of a dickhead, less arrogant, a more humble person, some sort of social agenda these days at least, realising one's own impotence, lack of control over events, all sorts of things Not that that would be enough reason to check in, but it certainly didn't do me any harm."

However, Marks also says "the just deserts bit of prison, the punishing, the revenge bit, I think that's disgusting." He also claims "prison is no deterrent at all. No one commits a crime, including the crimes I did, thinking they were going to get caught. The only deterrent is a very high detection rate. If the chances of getting busted are 99 per cent you're not going to do it."

This sounds a little odd, because surely, doing what he did, he must have known getting caught was likely at some point, and, indeed, he got caught more than once. "An awful lot of people don't get caught. I got caught because I was stupid. I kept telling everyone I was a dope dealer, did anyone want to buy it?" It's certainly true that if you want to evade the law, cooperating with a major biography of you by David Leigh, as Marks did, written while he was still in the business, wasn't the wisest move.

He may not read any philosophy these days, but its training may have stayed with Marks in less obvious ways. For instance, he agrees that it helps him articulate the case for legalisation of drugs, something he actively campaigns for, and actually stood for parliament on in 1997, shortly after his release from an American prison.

"One of the first proponents of the escalation argument, that those who take this are more likely to proceed to some other drug, was a professor of pharmacology at Oxford, Professor Paton. He showed all the statistics and everything and confirmed his hypothesis that if you take dope you're going to end up taking smack, but he'd actually got an incorrect application of Bayes' theorem. He made this elementary probabilist error in propounding the escalation argument which has had a tremendous effect on the world, you know, the gateway theory, all obviously complete bollocks, based on a professor's ineptitude in statistics."

So what is the case for legalisation? "To render cannabis less harmful to society than it is at the moment. I think it's that simple. I think the argument applies to every recreational drug so far discovered, certainly every one I've tried. One would have to allow for the possibility that someone either synthesises or discovers a drug that if you take it, it makes you kill people and rape them, that, yes, of course that should be illegal, whether it's natural or not. But I haven't come across one like that except possibly alcohol, the only one that is legal."

Many are attracted to the general idea but can't see how to practically make drugs available in ways that aren't potentially destructive, ▷▷▷

especially to the vulnerable. "I think it would depend a lot on the drug one is considering, and that should be linked to the relative harm of the drug. Professor David Nutt, the one who was sacked [as UK government drugs advisor], has a scale of harms, and one of his criteria for assessing the harm of any drug is the difference between the dose that gets you stoned and the dose that will kill you. If those two are very close then clearly that drug is dangerous in a way it wouldn't be if those doses were very different. So if one's tinkering around with something that, if you take a little too much, you're going to end up dead, yes, that can't be administered at a greengrocers. Cannabis could, whereas perhaps heroin ought to be administered by doctors."

"There are four main ways of distributing drugs. One is licensed premises, one is just ordinary retail markets, one is through the doctor and the other one is through organised crime. Why all the governments have decided on this last option as the way to do it, I don't know."

In the meantime, however, to get involved in the illegal sale of drugs means getting involved with some pretty unsavoury people. Marks says there's a different explanation for each. With the IRA, he says, "you have to remember that Harold Wilson sent in the army in 1969 to defend the Catholics. Sympathy for the Catholic minority in Northern Ireland was just part of the socialist agenda at the time."

When it comes to organised crime, Marks argues smuggling is no different from any other venture. "You go high enough in any business and you come across organised crime. You're going to run across the Mafia anyway. You're going to run across really corrupt bent people right at the top of the bankers." The only

difference, he claims, is that "You can have your blinkers on or not."

Nevertheless, his lifestyle certainly exacted a heavy price at times on his wife and children, whom he often says he adores in the book. "Oh it did, yeah, particularly the children. I think the psychological scars are still there. The kids went through what can only be called suffering." However, he says, "It's hard for me to regret anything now because I get on with my kids so well, they get on with me very well, we're all OK. It's very hard to regret your past if you're OK in the present – you don't want to risk changing anything."

Overall, would Marks say he has had a good life? Many people find it attractive and glamorous, but the hedonistic pursuit of altered states does not exactly get a good press in philosophy, which values staying as in touch with reality as possible.

"I don't think taking naturally growing herbs and substances takes one away from reality that much. Lots of experiences affect the mind. We are used to altered states from the days when we would spin around as kids just to get giddy, or have *puja* or baptism or go to a psychiatrist. We're used to altered states. Why there should be this prejudice against altered states of mind caused by chemicals I don't know."

And is philosophy going to feature in his future?

"It depends on whether I get nicked or not," he says, not for the first time breaking into a sincere and hearty laugh.

Mr Nice is published by Vintage Books in the UK and Minerva in the US

the skeptic

Psychic claimants and drug-addled egomaniacs

I cannot tell a lie. I have spent this weekend following the fortunes of the actor Charlie Sheen as he attempts a live tour. How does this relate to skeptics? Read on.

I rarely have any interest in celebrity gossip; I barely noticed Sheen's long history of drug busts, divorces, and lost cars. But I do have an interest in the workings of the entertainment business and the Internet, and when the highest-paid star in American TV comedy implodes in a series of bizarre rants and interviews and gets himself fired from his internationally successful show (*Two and a Half Men*), I get curious. Mostly about how the lawsuits are going to go, but somewhat about the people. Sheen's response to being fired from his $20 million-a-year job was to take his show on the road.

I was a full-time stage performer for six years (playing folk music, some of which you can hear at pelicancrossing.net/mp3s.htm), mostly playing for tiny audiences in obscure locations, so I do know a little about what it takes to play day after day in front of a live audience. The elements did not seem promising: an actor who, despite his skill and talent at creating characters written for him, is not a writer, comic or otherwise; has no history as a stage performer, let alone as a stand-up comic; and whose recent solo online appearances have been both incoherent and staggeringly arrogant.

As far as I can make out (from reports, Twitter feeds, and YouTube clips), Sheen was as incoherent as anyone had a right to expect. The first show, a mix of multimedia and ranting in Detroit, was disastrous; eager fans hoping for greatness wound up booing, walking out, and yelling for refunds. For the second show, in Chicago, Sheen changed to a straightforward interview format that at least kept the audience in their seats. My guess is that from here (there are at least twenty more dates to go) Sheen will become more polished, but the audiences will progressively shrink as more and more find the routine simply boring. Sheen comes across as a guy who prefers greatness or disaster to mediocrity; he may come to look back on that first Detroit night with fondness. (The good news is that the ticket scalpers will be the ones losing out most; many of the high-speed early ticket sales were not to folks spending their hard-earned money.)

So here's my point: to hold the attention of audiences night after night, year after year, you ⤐

Wendy M Grossman (pelicancrossing.net) is founder and former editor (twice) of *The Skeptic Magazine* (skeptic.org.uk)

last words/the skeptic

127

Angela George/Flickr

Charlie Sheen

laughter, or tears, it doesn't much matter which. Because the bar for success is set so high, psychics often begin by making efforts to lower expectations. They hope the spirits will cooperate tonight; they stress that their effects do not always work; they say they will need the audience's help and faith. Now (almost) everyone in the place is on the same side: they want the psychic to succeed.

Sheen, by contrast, did a terrible job with respect to audience expectations, hyping up what a great ("winning!") show it was going to be while giving barely a hint of what the show might actually be like. He antagonised the Detroit crowd early and often, telling an early heckler that "I've got your money". Worse, he lost control of himself and the situation.

Don't get me wrong: it took courage and professionalism to go out on stage that second night. Sheen was smart enough to recognise that he was not capable of keeping himself or the show coherent, and got one of the staff travelling with him to act as interviewer/referee/wrangler. Because ultimately that's the thing audiences do not forgive: the sense that the people on stage have lost control of the show. Experienced psychics don't lose that control: if anything, they have engineered the show in far more detail than the audience suspects. A drug-addled egomaniac, on the other hand, never had a lot of control to begin with, even if he had sufficient professional discipline to show up for work and ask the crew to move his marks so he'd have something to lean on when he was about to fall over.

have to have content, and it has to be well-timed and matched to the audience. So much is about context: the Chicago group had read the Detroit reviews and seen the clips. So they cheered, rather than jeered because: (i) the bar of expectation had now been set so low that the show *had* to be better, and (ii) it allowed them to be NOT-Detroit.

I have long held, for these reasons, that psychic claimants who perform regularly for large audiences are more likely to be frauds than those who see clients in small numbers, even if they charge for their services. The latter are far more likely to be deluded.

When you see psychic claimants performing in front of large audiences, all of these sorts of factors are at work. The audience hopes to see miracles – a message from a deceased loved one, a phenomenon they can't explain, a dramatic healing. They hope to be emotionally moved – to

128